Waiting on my Lunch Date

A Journey Through Grief and a Path to Joy

Gwendolyn Phillips Coates

PHILABOB PUBLISHING

A SUBSIDIARY OF GOD ANSWERS PRAYER MINISTRIES, INC.

Copyright © 2005 by Gwendolyn Phillips Coates
All rights reserved.
Printed in the United States of America

Published by Philabob Publishing
A subsidiary of God Answers Prayer Ministries, Inc.
Post Office Box 1682
Renton, WA 98057-1682

www.gap-ministries.com

Unless otherwise noted, all Scripture is from
The New King James Version.
Library of Congress Control Number: 2005903338
ISBN 0-9770187-0-9

DEDICATION

This book is dedicated to the memory of my late husband, the Rev. Leander Emanuel "Peter" Coates. He was the love of my life, and I will honor and treasure his memory forever.

I also honor the memory of my grandfathers, Rev. Henry Brooks and William Phillips (neither of whom I knew); grandmothers, Lena Van Randall and Mattie Brooks Green; uncles, Frank, George, Darwin, and Sam; aunts, Virginia, Bea, Dora Mae, Iola, and Viola; cousins, Bruce, Donna, Wanna, Michael, Kevin, and the McKinney twins; and friends Barbara Hunter, Rev. John Plummer, Jr. and Sis. Patricia Plummer.

I am grateful always to my two younger children, Philip and LaNicia, for their care and support during the most difficult time of our lives. Though Leander was not their biological father, the love and parent-child bond that was quickly established transcended a name on a birth certificate.

FOREWORD

Every person will become acquainted with grief and loss in his or her lifetime, whether dealing with the death of a loved one or the loss of a family home. Even though death is a natural part of normal lifespan development, death is often difficult to understand and accept. Furthermore, the inability to properly give oneself permission to go through the grieving process can also be problematic. Unfortunately, people can experience severe psychological and emotional distress because of unresolved grief and loss issues, causing them to require assistance from mental health professionals. Therefore, resources to help people to better cope with their grief and loss are indeed timely.

Several researchers, authors, and screenwriters have tackled this often confusing issue, but it is always delightful to find a resource that provides a personal perspective on the issue of death and dying. Sharing one's personal story is not only healing for the author, but it can be healing for the reader.

Waiting on my Lunch Date must certainly be added to the list of resources to assist people in dealing with their losses and finding joy in the midst of sorrow. Rev. Gwendolyn Phillips Coates, the author shares her love story, along with the personal struggles and triumphs she experienced while attempting to make sense of the death of her husband. Rev. Coates has a unique way of integrating the tragedy, with humor and spiritual antidotes, which helps to create life and hope for those who may otherwise feel hopeless in their grief.

This thoughtful book brings to life the agony of coming to terms with the loss of someone you love, and it helps the reader to put into words all the thoughts, feelings, and behaviors that are common to only those who share the loss. Waiting on my Lunch Date elicits all the range of emotions, from tears to laughter, and by the end of the book, the reader will find him or herself encouraged because of the spiritual strategies that are shared to promote inner healing.

If you are a man or woman who has lost a loved one, or anything you hold near and dear to your heart, this book is for you. It does not matter if you have suffered a recent loss, or if you are suffering from an unresolved grief and loss issue, this book was written for you. In fact, this book was written by you. It is easy to read, but most of all easy to relate to. As you will learn from the story as told by Rev. Gwendolyn Coates, there is life on the other side. Your loved one will never be forgotten, but you can live again.

—Gloria Morrow, Ph.D.
Licensed Clinical Psychologist
President, GM Psychological Services
Upland, California

CONTENTS

Acknowledgements / viii

Preface / xi

PART ONE:
THE JOURNEY THROUGH GRIEF

Chapter 1   Every Moment Counts / 2

Chapter 2   66 Days / 9
            Waiting / 15
            God Is Right / 25

Chapter 3   Rainy Days and Thursdays / 31
            Thank God for Green Beans / 34

Chapter 4   Functioning but Not Feeling / 37
            More Than Tears / 39

Chapter 5   Suddenly Single / 42
            Widow / 44
            I Miss You / 47

PART TWO:
THE PATH TO JOY

Chapter 6   Permission to Mourn / 52
            Joy Comes in the Morning / 57

Chapter 7   Discovering a New Normal / 65
             Taking Self from the Shelf / 73

Chapter 8   Promoting A Healthy You / 77
             Flying Solo / 78

PART THREE:
SPIRITUAL STRENGTH FOR
THE HURTING SOUL

Chapter 8   Help Me Make It Through the Night / 86

Chapter 9   Mourning to Dancing / 92

Chapter 10   A New Beginning / 94
             When Morning Comes / 95

ACKNOWLEDGEMENTS

I thank God for giving me the mind, heart and inspiration to share from my heart, the tragedy of loss that has plagued our family. The gift of writing should be listed in the wonderful healing gifts God provides.

I have so many people to thank. The support (both tangible and intangible), love, guidance and understanding during this process have been remarkable. I owe a debt of gratitude to so many who have helped shape me. The writing of this book has grown from an idea to what you now hold in your hands.

I am so grateful to have found a gifted, knowledgeable and proficient editor, Barbara Fandrich. I know a treasure when I see one. Thanks for being a precious jewel.

Throughout this journey my biggest cheerleaders have been my family. I am so blessed and my heart is full of gratitude. My sister, Dr. Gloria Phillips Morrow has lead the way, waving the victory banner for this project. Her encouragement kept me focused on writing during the many days and nights when I wanted to quit because of painful memories. I would not have completed this book without your constant reminders of the ultimate goals. Thanks.

I thank my parents Rev. Harold and Mrs. Henrietta Phillips who still believe that I can accomplish great things.

My younger children LaNicia and Philip have provided unconditional love, constant companionship and shared in the embryonic stages of development and subsequent birth of this book. I thank and appreciate you for sharing me with the computer and understanding my many mood swings during this process. Thanks to Bobby, Michella and Mikkel for understanding my decrease in trips to Houston. See you soon.

To my brother-in-law Rev. Tommy Morrow, brothers and sisters-in-law Charlie Powell (LaVonne), Harold Wayne Phillips (Lisa), Randy Cornell Phillips (Sheila), my aunts, uncle, cousins, nieces, nephews —our family is what it is because we are all in it. You have always cheered for my best good. Thank you.

Thank you to my many sistah-friends (and brothers) Leola Andrews Pride (Charles), Pat Watts, Jackie Calloway (Kelvin), Gwendolyn Foster-Steen (Ellerd), Dori Williams, Rev. Shermella Garrett, and Carolyn Scott Brown (Lester) for proving that love is a bloodline. Friends are the family we choose and I choose you. Thanks for the shoulder of support. I am here for you, too. To the Rainbow Group of widows that traveled to Jamaica in November 2003, thank you for letting me learn from you. All of us are on the path of *new beginnings*. I pray you arrive safely at your new destinations of your journey.

To my wife-in-law, Forrestine "Flo" Jacobs, you know I love you girl. We have the most unusual relationship. I am so glad Ernest found you. You have been a great mother to Phil (and LaNicia). We became widows six weeks apart and have helped one another so much during this season of grief. I wish you much happiness with your new love.

To my church family, the warm, wonderful and winsome folks of Walker Chapel AME, you have blessed my life immensely. Thank you for walking with me while on the journey of a lifetime. I pray that our time together is well spent and God will continue to grow us in love, relationship and ministry. I am additionally grateful to Rev. Jonathon and Sis. Margaret Rhone and the St. John, Bethel, Allen and Gregg Memorial AME church families in Omaha, Nebraska for remembering and being so hospitable to us.

Thank you Rev. Dr. Cecil L. "Chip" Murray for saying to me in 1992, "You must write." You have been a great influence in my life.

Bishop John Richard Bryant and Rev. Cecelia Williams Bryant, thank you for your prayers, thoughtfulness and concern during the time I have known you. Rev. C, thanks for encouraging me to heal. I honor the wisdom of both you and Bishop John. To the presiding elders, pastors, ministers and laity of the Fifth Episcopal District of the African Methodist Episcopal Church, thank you for being my Aaron's when I was too weak to lift my arms. I truly appreciate all of the support and encouragement shown toward me. I am grateful to all the pastors of the Pacific Northwest Conference and retired Presiding Elder Ellis Casson for making the ICU waiting room of Harbor View Medical Center—*Holy Ground*. Your presence, prayers and words of encouragement sustained us.

A special thank you to those of you who kept extended vigils with us at Harbor View Medical Center, Sisters Audrey Miller, Dorothy Johnson and Denise Hunter.

Please forgive me in advance if you feel your name should be listed and I have inadvertently omitted it. I am providing the following space so that you might insert your name and know that I honor you as well.

_____

PREFACE

*"If you get there before I do, tell all my friends
I'm coming too!"*

My life changed abruptly and permanently on November 29, 2001. The events of the day are forever etched in my memory, and life never will be the same for my immediate family or me. The day started out as any other day. Who will take our son to school? What kinds of things are we doing today? What do you want for breakfast? What will we do for dinner tonight? And, "Can I take you to lunch?"

I left home the morning of November 29, 2001 happy and in love. My husband and I had just shared a very passionate and loving morning together. He had insisted that I stay in bed while he took our son to school. When he returned we played around a bit, got up, showered, dressed, and prepared breakfast. I fussed at him because he was preparing to eat a banana, reminding him that the doctors had told him not to eat bananas. His reply was that they'd told him to eat potatoes instead, which he considered to be so boring. However, he promised me that this would be the last banana he would eat. And it was.

This book is written to help those who are going through grief due to the death of a spouse. As I go through the healing process, I am sharing my story and hoping it will be a blessing to others who have faced this situation. I hope anyone reading this book will be encouraged as the grief process takes its own form in his or her life. This book is also intended to create a spark in the lives of husbands and wives. None of us know when our relationship will be broken by death. My story of loss and grief should encourage couples to reevaluate and appreciate their relationship.

I never thought about becoming a widow. It has taken me totally by surprise. I, like most widows, didn't plan for my husband to die. In fact, we used to joke about being raptured together, or holding hands and saying to the Lord, "Lord, we're ready. Take us both now." We were still on our honeymoon, and would have remained in this state of bliss for the next fifty years. But God has spoken, and I accept God's will.

This event has had a tremendous effect on my personal well being. My life, health, and attitude have been altered because of the death of my husband. You may be able to relate to some of the pain described in this book. I must admit that some of the pain was intensified by my actions. I tried drowning my pain and sorrow by filling all my waking hours with as much activity as possible. I have given new meaning to the word "workaholic." If you've experienced loss and have kept moving, going, and working you'll find, as I did, that no matter what we do: work, travel, or sleep, grief is always waiting for us when we stop.

The death of Leander has created an eternal pause in my life that has placed me on hold in a waiting pattern. We didn't say "Goodbye." We said, "See you at two." The fact that two o'clock came and went without the lunch date has created an unimaginable season of disbelief in my mind. This feeling of waiting is like being placed on a shelf or in limbo. Only Leander can engage the mechanism to put me back in my rightful place. This state has intensified the shocking effects of his passing.

In this book I will retell my story and attempt to unpack the feelings and emotions trapped in the space of my heart and mind while waiting. I will also recommend a way to rediscover life on the other side of grief that will lead to a path of joy. Remember, the time it takes to work through grief is individual. If this book helps in any way to lessen the sting of loss, my job will be "well done."

As you read these pages you will have a personal encounter with the Reverends Leander and Gwendolyn Coates, our family, extended family, and friends. This is the story of my journey through grief and path to joy. I could not have made this journey by myself. My family, extended family, friends, and foes comforted me the best they could. But, I would not have survived this phase of my life without my faith and strong relationship with my Lord and Savior, Jesus Christ. So I've included the final section of this book entitled "Spiritual Strength for the Hurting Soul."

Take courage, be strong, take a deep breath, and let the journey begin.

PART 1

The Journey Through Grief

CHAPTER 1

Every Moment Counts

On September 11, 2001 the United States of America had a very devastating blow. This attack on America resulted in the death of thousands of people. Many wives became widows, husbands became widowers, children became orphans, and families became grievers.
CONFIRMED DEAD: 2948
REPORTED DEAD: 24
REPORTED MISSING: 24
TOTAL: 2996

I CONTINUE TO PRAY for all of the widows/widowers and children left without parents, families, and all those affected by the horrific attack on America, September 11, 2001. My heart goes out to those whose loved ones' voices were silenced by a savage act. Our family's heart was wrenched on September 11th for several nerve-wracking hours. For us, our loved one was safe on that day and finally returned home to us. Less than three months later we suffered the ultimate loss and felt the sorrow and grief that losing a loved one can cause.

Shortly before the attacks of September 11, on August 26, 2001, Leander and I were told we were both being relocated from Omaha, Nebraska, to the Pacific Northwest. We were each Itinerant Elders in the African Methodist Episcopal church. The Itinerancy literally means "traveling pastor," and that is the legal term used to move pastors from one church to another. This can include being moved from one city or state to another city or state. And this was the case for us. Leander had pastored Bethel AME Church in Omaha for three years and was now receiving a promotion. Actually, both of us were receiving a promotion, as I would soon become pastor of Walker Chapel AME Church in Seattle, but Leander's was on another level of ministry. He would be the presiding elder of the Pacific Northwest Conference, a supervisory role overseeing churches, and a position that reports directly to the bishop. His assignment would begin September 1, 2001 and mine would begin October 29.

Leander's instructions were to go to his assignment immediately. His position required immediate attention, and there was a need for his expeditious arrival. I made his travel arrangements right away so we could get the best possible airfare available with short notice.

He was so excited—and he had every right to be. No matter what line of work we are in, it is always exciting to go the next level. Even in ministry, to receive a promotion is a wonderful feeling. Additionally, he was to be the first presiding elder appointment given by The Right Rev. John Richard Bryant, Presiding Prelate of the Fifth District in the African Methodist Episcopal Church.

Leander always wanted to minister in the Pacific Northwest. He felt in his spirit that this was where God wanted him to be. The position he would fill had been vacated in August, and Leander was told to go immediately to this new assignment. This would be the second assignment of this type for Leander. Prior to our marriage he had served in this capacity in the Colorado Conference, Rocky Mountain District. The Pacific Northwest Conference encompasses four states: Alaska, Montana, Oregon, and Washington. Since the greatest number of churches is in Washington and near Seattle, he immediately planned to go to Seattle. We would also plan to live in this area, so part of his plan would be to secure housing for us, meet with the pastors, then return to Omaha for our move.

Moving can be such a hassle, but we were excited about moving to the West Coast. We believed the West Coast has so much to offer, whether it is north or south. We were glad to be going to a little warmer climate. The frigid winters in the Midwest can take a toll on you. And you never get used to it. We felt that somehow the opportunities would be endless; we'd meet new people, start new ministries, and grow slumping ones. This was going to be a chance of a lifetime for us. So our family got on the same page and we began making plans to come west.

During Leander's absence, I would tidy up loose ends, find moving companies and construct a plan for continuing my pastoral ministry in Omaha. We began notifying friends and extended family of our new assignment and the opportunity for new ministry. Even though we were concerned that our youngest son, Phil, would be leaving Omaha at a crucial point, we knew everything would work out. This was his senior year in high school. He was concerned about making new friends, keeping his grades up, and adapting to a new school environment. But those fears soon waned as we discussed the new frontier that we could conquer together.

Leander's itinerary would have him leave September 5, 2001 around 7 am with a return flight on September 11, 2001 at 6:45 am PST. I remember taking my daughter to work that morning. In Omaha there is a television station that is also on the radio, so in the car we kept our radio station tuned to this station because we wanted to be informed of any immediate changes in the traffic conditions or the weather. It was also nice to keep up with some of the TV shows while driving. This particular Tuesday morning, as I dropped my daughter off, I remember a commercial being interrupted by Katie Couric of *Good Morning America*. She was speaking with a frantic woman on the telephone. It took a moment to realize what was going on because I was listening, not watching. The woman began to say it appeared that a plane collided with the World Trade Center in New York.

I still did not understanding the full impact. I halfway listened while continuing with my day. My usual routine on many Tuesday mornings was to head for the opening of the store named "Tuesday Morning," and this morning was no different. I stopped to shop for Tuesday morning specials. While I was in the store other shoppers came in expressing disbelief and shock from the news that two planes had collided with the Twin Towers in New York, and I suddenly realized something was very wrong. I left my shopping cart in the aisle and went directly home, where members of our church family had already begun calling me to see if Leander was OK.

I began calling Leander's cell phone, even though I knew he was already in route. I wanted him to hear from me, and I left message after message leaving him updates on America's condition and position. Shortly after that, all planes in the United States were grounded, meaning no planes were allowed to enter the air. All planes en route were ordered to land in the nearest possible airfield.

To my great relief, I finally got a call from Leander. He told me the airline personnel had told them America was under attack, and they had to land as soon as possible. They landed the plane in Spokane, Washington, but because there was no terminal (for the airline he was traveling on), all passengers from his plane would be transported back to Seattle by bus.

I was so glad to hear his voice. He wanted to get off the phone and listen to the announcements that were being made, but I wanted him to stay on the phone with me. He had not seen the images of the terror that was creating havoc in New York. I had. So my need to have and keep communication with him was confusing to him. Once he got to a television, he totally understood.

All of us were shocked and bewildered by the tragic events of this day. All of us have prayed for the families and loved ones affected by this tragedy. I did not totally experience the full effect of losing someone when this event occurred, but being out of touch with my husband for several hours on that day was a very uncomfortable feeling.

I remember watching the televised images and seeing the horrific scenes of the planes becoming one with the Twin Towers. It was overwhelming to watch the Twin Towers become rubble and dust right before our eyes. No one who witnessed the tragic events and images of September 11, 2001 will ever forget them.

The ban on flying finally lifted later that week, and Leander finally made it back to my arms on Friday. I could not forget the unbearable ache in my heart when I couldn't reach him for those few hours on September 11th. Not knowing how this would turn out for our family was a wrenching reality. We asked ourselves, "Will he be caught up in the rage of the terrorists? Will the planes suspend their grounded status soon? When will he come home? Is America safe?" You might ask, is it safe today?

When Leander arrived home we were like newlyweds again. No disagreements, no harsh words, no sharp tones. We made the most of every moment. Prior to the September 11th experience we were close, but we became closer. More hand-holding, more kisses, and more special moments. We made every moment count. We began calling each other on our cell phones just to say, "I love you," and "I miss you," or "Hurry home."

Life goes on. Unfortunately and way too soon, we got back to somewhat normal lives. I was scheduled to preach at a revival in Riverside, California, September 19 to 21. My family in California tried to convince me to cancel it, but I believed that it was the right time to go. I believed this was the safest time to travel because everyone was on high alert. Planes were on time. Because many people were afraid to fly, airports were less crowded. Most people were patient because they were more afraid of not being safe than of the time spent going through airport security's new procedures. When we parted at the airport I remember longer hugs and kisses, calling one another after getting past security, staying on the phone until boarding, and ending the conversation with a promise to call as soon as the plane landed. All this because we had become keenly aware that every moment counts. We all knew we were more vulnerable.

Checking in became routine and the norm for us. We would call each other once we changed locations and arrived at our destination. We would call and say, "Just checkin' in." Sometimes we would make these calls and not be going anywhere at all. It was as though an alarm went off inside of us if we hadn't heard from each other within a certain span of time, and one of us would make a "just checkin' in" call. It's amazing how our desire to know the moves of our significant other was once seen as distrust for an independent lifestyle. Keeping tabs on each other meant I need to know where you are at all times, and this cramped our style. There was a time that I was highly insulted if someone wanted to know my every move. I was indignant if I had to surrender my schedule and agenda for the day to someone of the opposite sex. My parents told me that I'd been independent all my life. I didn't like being fussed with as a newborn. Just let me be. Let me do my own thing. And as the years rolled on, I became more independent with each birthday. Coupled with being a rebel by nature and having a need to feel free, my surrendering to "checkin' in" was a big thing. I don't even know how it happened. It just emerged, and the next thing I knew, I had transferred it from my husband to the children, and then to my parents, siblings, church members, and friends. Everybody has to "check in."

I have discovered that "just checkin' in" is more that just a way to keep tabs on a person. It actually is a wonderful communication booster. The more you speak with loved ones, family and friends, the more you know one another, and the closer you become as a result. When we discover that every moment counts, we see how valuable and precious every moment is, especially after our loved ones are gone and all we have are memories. This little slang phrase also means so much more. It means love you, miss you, thinking about you, and wishing you were here. It also means I'm sorry, let bygones be bygones, or are you still mad? Sometimes checkin' in is really checking to see if the tone of voice has changed or if the attitude is in need of adjustment.

We continued with our plans to move to Seattle. September 29 we loaded up the cars, and the family drove west to Seattle.

CHAPTER 2

66 ays

WE ARRIVED IN THE STATE of Washington October 1, 2001. The drive from Omaha, Nebraska to Washington was beautiful. The landscape changed right before our eyes. The Midwest is very flat with lots of cornfields. What a contrast as we continued to drive west. The West is very beautiful country with mountains, hills, streams, waterfalls, and lots of trees. I can remember the most beautiful sunrises and sunsets. The color of the sky would change to gorgeous hues of blue and purple, and golden tones with auburn burn-off that only God can create. The golden and reddish shades of the trees signaled the season changing, but for the most part, everything was evergreen. The early morning mists and vapors would rise and surround the trees, creating an image shrouded in low clouds, then suddenly, as we were driving up a hill, the sun would make its appearance. We were in awe of the magnificence and majesty of God's handiwork. We were so grateful to be able to see this beauty, if only for a moment.

We traveled west in two cars. Our newer Nissan Altima and an older Ford Taurus. My younger two children (then sixteen and twenty-three) were licensed drivers, and we took turns switching cars and drivers. Leander had more patience with our youngest son who had only been licensed for less than a year. So when Phil was driving, Leander was his road dog. None of us could've imagined the fun we'd have driving across country. The weather was perfect. We barely saw a cloud in the sky, and if we did see clouds they were surrounded by beautiful blue sky. We clung to one another and even called each other on our cell phones during our drive if one car experienced a thought or a sighting that had to be shared. Many times we'd experience a weak signal from our phones and we couldn't wait to share the information with one another at the next food, coffee, gas, or bathroom stop.

Looking back, I reflect upon how happy we all were to be together. My daughter and I wore no makeup, our clothes were casual, and we didn't care if the wind mussed our hair; we were just glad to be together. We played music, sang along, swapped CDs between cars, swayed to the beats, and loved each other's company. For those few days on the road, we escaped the cares of the world and experienced family. We were making every moment count in ways we hadn't done before. Phil and Leander had great bonding time and shared a lot of father-son talk in the hours they were road buddies. LaNicia and I had wonderful mother-daughter time. When LaNicia and Phil were together, they were the wild, wonderful kids they are. And Leander and I were grateful when the two of us got to talk mushy to each other without the ears of our young people.

At every hotel, pit stop, café and rest stop, we were lovin' this new experience and making the most of our time together. We were on a new adventure and we knew it was going to be wonderful. Not without a struggle, but wonderful nonetheless. We were encouraged by the faith our bishop had in us to do a new thing in a new place for our good and God's glory. We were thoughtful and hopeful about all the new realities we would face. In our last assignment in Omaha we would frequently say, "I don't know what God is doing, but I want God to continue doing what He is doing." We had experienced a wonderful, exciting ministry in Omaha. It is a place where people love the Lord, love the church experience, and usually love their pastors.

In Omaha we had been busy in our churches, community, and schools. We were very politically involved, too, and we stayed on the go. We were preaching at other churches, traveling to nearby cities to minister, meeting new people all the time, and sharing on many different levels with people we met. Leander was president of the Ministerial Alliance and this gave him a seat at most spiritual and secular negotiation tables, from civil rights to the mayor and/or governor's office. We were constantly being asked to attend meetings geared toward defending and protecting the rights of the disenfranchised. Whenever we were called, if we could, we would go. Hospitals, mortuaries, churches, schools, protests, rallies, you name it. When the call came, we were there. Not in the back or on the periphery, but right up front waving the banner for liberty and justice for all.

Before going to Washington, we didn't examine the conditions we were going to face, but with our prior track record, we were ready to tackle the good, the bad, and the ugly head on. We didn't research the new place we would call home. Not even the weather conditions and patterns. We did, however, listen to a lot of so-called "informants" and discovered after our own experience that they were not in the least bit correct. Everybody says that it rains a lot in Seattle. That was the assumption we moved there with. Actually, it doesn't rain as much as people think it does. We were told that Washington had the highest number of suicide victims in the U.S. However, we found this to be untrue also. Washington ranks around sixteenth in the nation. One of the major causes is the number of rainy and/or gray days. We were not told how low Washington ranked in reference to church attendance. In a poll taken in 1999, Washington State ranked the lowest in the country for people who attend church on a regular basis. I'm glad we didn't know that in advance; however, it has proven to be true.

So we arrived in Washington to beautiful weather and a gorgeous skyline, weary from a cross-country road trip. We stayed in a hotel that first night, and the next day we saw the house Leander and one of the pastors in Washington had chosen for us. We never lived in that house, however, for reasons you'll see shortly.

While he was in Washington in September 2001, he and one of the pastors went house hunting and found the ugliest house in Washington. Well, maybe that's a little extreme, but he managed to find a house with navy blue carpet and navy blue walls. I think the yellow leather furniture of the previous occupant fooled him. I really tried to act as though I could love the house, but I really didn't. It was too dark, there was the smell of dogs (I had an immediate allergic reaction), the closet was 2-foot by 2-foot, and the bedroom wasn't big enough for two people and a bed. It just wasn't going to work. I privately asked the Lord to help me find a way to tell my husband I didn't want to live in the house he had chosen, without hurting his feelings. I'd only seen the house on the Internet. It looked like a nice house online. It's hard to estimate room sizes from a photo. But my honey had picked it out and I thought I could leave the decision up to him. Wrong! He somehow sensed my disapproval, and the next morning he suggested we find a paper and look at other houses—hallelujah! We did and the right house was waiting for us. It had enough space, adequate room sizes, and the closets were sufficient. The Lord even made a way for us to take possession of it right away. We did all this without knowing the geography of the Seattle area. We probably would've picked somewhere closer to Seattle had we known, but we moved in based on our anticipated pleasure of this new place. We found a wonderful five bedroom, five bath house in Kent, Washington. It resembled a home I once owned in Redondo Beach, California. It was as though the Lord was giving us a second chance to enjoy this house. I had lost the California home due to mismanagement of money by a former spouse. I later went through an ugly divorce, but God is faithful—five years later I married the right man. We always joked about how wonderful it might've been had we met fifteen, twenty, even twenty-five years earlier. We would have had more time to love each other.

We took possession the next day. Our furniture hadn't arrived yet, so we purchased sleeping bags and slept on the floor for the next five days. The house had a built-in stove and oven, so at least we were able to cook. There was a refrigerator, so we found the local grocery store and began filling the refrigerator with our favorite goodies. We didn't have a table, so I went to the local thrift store and found a glass-top table for $25, which I covered with a beautiful tablecloth from a local discount store. Then I went to another thrift store and found four chairs for $3 each—and when I was through we had a suitable family dinner table for less than $50. This table was later passed down to my daughter when she moved into her own apartment.

Our furniture finally arrived on October 8, one week after we arrived in Washington and five days after we settled into our new home. Once the gigantic moving truck arrived, we were once again convinced we had made the right choice for our living space. We found later on that many of the houses in the Seattle area have very small rooms. It was wonderful to live in a comfortable place where everything fit and everyone had his or her own space. I have yet to find a house anywhere with enough closet space, but that's a whole other issue.

By us not knowing the geographical makeup of Washington, we had selected a home that was about forty-five minutes from Seattle in Kent, on the East Hill. This suburb of Seattle is a wonderful, clean, newly developed area. In fact when we moved in, the main street leading to our new home hadn't been paved yet.

We'd thoroughly enjoyed our new adventure so far. Initially, I was traveling back to Omaha for the first six weeks after our arrival in Washington. My new assignment would not be announced for several weeks, and I would not know until October 29 exactly which church I would be pastoring. It didn't matter. We were excited to be on the West Coast. Leander's dream of coming to the Pacific Northwest was finally a reality, and we were waiting to see God's next move. Finally, on October 29 in Oakland, California, I received my assignment to pastor Walker Chapel AME Church in Seattle, Washington. This congregation had seen many struggles over the years, and I had my work cut out for me. I wasn't worried though because I knew that with God's help this new congregation and I would do great things for the Kingdom of God.

The next few days and weeks after our arrival in the Seattle area were a whirlwind of activity. Getting settled in a new house, moving into my office, meeting all the membership, preparing sermons and bible studies . . . what an exciting time. I was really looking forward to this new ministry opportunity and was ready for the challenge. It really helped that we were already moved into our new house so there would be no delay in settling into my new assignment.

Our son Phil got enrolled as a senior at Kentwood High School; LaNicia decided to move back to California after a couple of weeks, and Leander and I began our work. The move had taken a toll on both of us physically, so we made appointments with doctors in the area and transferred our medical records. I cancelled my appointments due to scheduling conflicts, but Leander kept his. We searched for and found grocery stores, nail salons, pedicure operators, hair stylists, barber shops, and of course the malls. We found the shopping outlets, army and air force bases for transferring our medical records, and auto mechanics, and then we were set for a while. We adapted to our schedules quickly so there was no lapse in our work. Everything was falling into place, and we were ready.

Leander's job description included traveling to the fourteen churches in his district that spanned the four state territory of Washington, Oregon, Montana, and Alaska. This meant most Sundays he would be at a different church. We decided he would become a member of a church other than Walker Chapel, Seattle. We didn't want the membership to get confused and think they had two pastors. I suggested and he agreed not to discuss church business in the car or the house (particularly the bedroom). All supervisor/pastor meetings between us would be by appointment and take place either at the church or at a restaurant. I even suggested to him that one of his colleagues serve as an intermediary between us if church issues got in the way of love issues. I wasn't about to ruin my marriage because of church problems. We had a job, a plan, and a mission. And we were going to show the Lord that we appreciated His faithfulness toward us by doing His will to the best of our ability.

On November 29, 2001 I had two afternoon appointments. One with a musician, and another with the chairperson of a church committee. The musician's meeting didn't take long, but it was a delightful meeting. I was very impressed that this young man took the initiative to share with me his feelings about his musical ability, and that he offered to step aside if I found another musician. After his departure, I began preparing for the next meeting and prepared an agenda for the meeting scheduled for later that evening. Then my second appointment canceled, meaning our lunch date time could be moved up and Leander and I would have more time together. I began trying to reach him. The rest of the events of that day changed my life forever. Day 59.

Waiting

Waiting. Waiting...What do you do while you're waiting?

On Wednesday, November 28, 2001, Leander made it home before I did. I taught my usual Bible study class that night, and when I arrived home, he was sitting in a chair reading the Bible. When I walked through the bedroom door he was so glad to see me. He immediately turned his attention to me. We kissed hello, as usual, and began to discuss the events of the day. His day was rather light. He'd picked Phil up from school and just chilled (relaxed) until I got home. He appeared to be fine. We turned in for the evening and continued with our Wednesday night ritual of watching *Soul*

Food on Showtime. As the scenes were rolling and Bird and Lem were having their usual spats, Leander took me in his arms, kissed my forehead, and said to me, "Baby, I love you." I said, "I know." He responded, "I really love you." And I countered, "I really know." We chuckled and cuddled, and I warmed my cold feet on his legs as we continued watching our show. We fell asleep in each other's arms.

Thursday, November 29, 2001 was a very loving morning for Leander and me. We woke up with our usual morning chatter. Noticing it was time to take Phil to school, I started to get out of bed. Phil was a senior in high school and still had the luxury of his parents or sister taking him to school and picking him up. As I leaned on my side to get out of bed, Leander insisted that I stay in bed and he would take Phil to school. When he returned, we had a very loving and passionate time together. We took our time, even though both of us had a work schedule for the day. He suggested we go to lunch after his meeting and in between my meetings. I told him I'd arrange for one of the members of the church to pick Phil up from school so we'd be free to spend lunchtime together.

We then showered, dressed, and had breakfast, which for me was coffee and a small bowl of cereal. Leander had coffee, toast, and cereal. Then he grabbed a banana and began removing the peel as he stood at the kitchen sink. I reminded him that his doctor had told him to stop eating bananas, and now he was about to have another one. Earlier that month, after a doctor visit, he'd shared with me that his diet would have to change. He was diabetic and overweight. I knew he'd been eating whatever he wanted, but both of us had recently agreed to start taking better care of ourselves. So, he told me he'd stop eating bananas. He said the doctor told him to eat potatoes instead, but he wasn't pleased with that substitution. Laughingly he said, "This is going to be my last banana." And it was.

Before leaving home that morning we called my brother Randy to tell him happy birthday. Then I showed him how to log on to the Internet to see pictures of his newborn grandson by his daughter in Utah. Everything appeared to be normal. Normal conversation, normal exclamations, everything seemed to be normal. Leander did complain of a slight headache, but we just kind of brushed it off. So I prepared to leave with the understanding that I'd see him at two o'clock. I kissed him and took my things to the car. After placing my books and briefcase on the back seat of the car, I opened the garage and did something unusual. I went back into the house and kissed him again. That would be the last kiss we shared.

My day changed when my one o'clock appointment canceled. I immediately began trying to reach Leander on his cell phone. This would mean we could go to lunch earlier and have more time together prior to my next meeting that evening. I knew he had a meeting that morning with a local pastor and would probably not have his phone accessible, so I left him a very loving message. "Honey, my one o'clock appointment cancelled, and I'll be ready for lunch whenever you are. We get to spend more time together. Love you."

Waiting!

Fifteen minutes later I tried again. "Honey, please call me as soon as you get this message."

WAITING! Waiting, waiting. I finally began to get impatient and the tone of my messages changed. I knew that Leander had business with one of the ministers who was arriving by plane that day. The procedure in the AME church is that our bishop appoints us all to our churches, and the term of our assignment is one year at a time. We receive a certificate that bears the seal of the African Methodist Episcopal Church and the signature of our bishop. This is a very important document because it is read to the congregation, usually on the first Sunday following the new minister's appointment. One of the pastors was ill when his appointment was made, and it was Leander's responsibility on this day to make sure this document was in his hands.

I began to rationalize Leander's steps in order to figure out why he had not answered any of my calls. I know that sometimes congregations prepare a meal when they are receiving a new pastor and/or presiding elder. So I began to see in my mind's eye that Leander would graciously pick at a small plate of food, knowing that he and I would meet for lunch later. I could envision him as he looked at his caller ID on his cell phone, noted my number, and decided not to answer but to get back to me as soon as possible. I didn't like this imaginary scenario, but I accepted it. This helped the waiting process.

I don't like waiting. In this modern world with all the forms of modern technological communication devises, we really don't have to wait to get in touch with people we love. The previous year for Valentine's Day I had given the gift of communication to Leander, Phil, and LaNicia. Each of them received a cell phone as my gift to them. And since that time our service provider had upgraded the communication system so that we could reach each other on our cell phones without using precious minutes. It cost us a little more, but with our phone plan we can call one another as often as we want to.

All right. It's been an hour now, and Leander hasn't called me back. This is very unlike him. He is always very prompt. Even though he says he doesn't like the telephone, he calls me at least every hour just to say "I love you," or "Thinking about you," or "What are you doing?" And now time is passing with no communication from him.

The time is growing closer to his meeting me at the church. I am anticipating his arrival. I'll just freshen my lipstick, even though he'll kiss me and mess it up. I bet he's bringing me flowers. He hasn't brought flowers for me at the church yet. That's what he's been up to. He didn't call me back because he wouldn't be able to keep the surprise from me that he was out buying flowers.

Then suddenly, without any warning I got this pain in my stomach that signaled to my brain that something was wrong. This was more than hunger, this was my beginning to feel my husband's energy and sense there was a problem. I began calling his cell phone again, feeling that if he'd had an accident perhaps the paramedics or the police would hear it ringing and would answer his phone. *Why isn't somebody picking up?* I prayed and asked God to take care of him and the situation. I prayed and prayed right there at my desk in the office of the church. The more I prayed, the more my spirit and my senses became aware that something was terribly wrong.

This lack of communication was so out of character for Leander. I called his cell phone again, and then I began calling the house, but no one answered. I was becoming quite concerned. I began knowing in my heart that there was a problem. When you have a relationship with the Lord, it's amazing how God just begins to move us in a path of understanding through our feelings. I knew something was wrong. I kept praying and asking the Lord to let everything be all right. Not hearing from Leander within this time span was so out of character, but I really didn't know where to begin looking.

My stomach began growling. I'd only had a bowl of cereal that morning, and I was waiting on my lunch date to eat a more satisfying meal. I knew it was getting close to the time that Phil would be getting home from school. I kept calling the house until Phil finally answered the phone. I tried to stay calm. I didn't want to alarm him without a reason. I'd just ask him a few questions to see if he knew anything about Leander's whereabouts.

Phil was his usual self. He answered my questions. Yes, Gene Harden had picked him up from school. Yes, he'd gone to get something to eat on his way home. Yes, he'd had a good day at school. He was hungry and was eating while trying to quickly get me off the phone. I got his attention and asked him if when he arrived home, he'd seen his dad's car in the driveway. At first he said no (whew—some relief), but then he said, "As a matter of fact I did." I thank God for the presence of mind that He gave me to instruct Phil to go upstairs to my bedroom and see if he was OK. I don't know why, but the Lord instructed me to tell Phil exactly where to go. When Phil got to the top of the stairs and turned toward our bedroom, he began screaming "Oh no! P.C., get up! P.C., are you all right?" I immediately told Phil to call 911. I told him I would hang up, run to my car, and call him back on my cell phone. My first thought was that Leander must have had another heart attack. He'd had a mild heart attack in May of 2000 and since that time had not continued on the recommended regimen of weight loss, physical activity, and reducing stress from his life. I also knew that he'd had difficulty getting on the Internet that morning and had said he'd try to call his daughter if he couldn't log on. I didn't know if this would have been a stressful conversation or if he was tired or just sick.

As I negotiated the steps of the church and moved toward my car, the Lord gave me a message in an audible voice saying, "Leander is gone." I can remember hearing my voice reply, "No Lord, I'm not ready!" I got into the car, called Phil back on the cell phone, and found the paramedics were already there trying to revive Leander. While Phil was on the phone with me I can remember hearing him talk to Leander telling him to hang in there, telling him he loved him, reassuring him he was going to be all right. Phil gave the phone to the paramedics and I began walking them through our bedroom to find Leander's medication, telling them Leander's medical history (as I knew it), his birthday and place of birth, answering questions as I kept driving. I could hear them saying, "Sir? Sir?" and calling his name trying to get some response but I couldn't hear Leander's voice. I couldn't hear him. And I never heard his voice again.

The paramedics came back to the telephone to inform me they would need to airlift Leander to Harbor View Medical Center. They would not be able to land a helicopter on our street because of the telephone and cable wires in the area. They would need to transport him by ambulance to a nearby high school and transport him from there. When they gave me this information and ended our conversation, I immediately exited the freeway, made a U-turn in the middle of the intersection and headed back to the nearest freeway onramp. I knew I needed to go back to Seattle, but I didn't know where I was or how to get where I was going. The night before I had programmed one of the member's phone number in my phone. I hoped she was home so she could direct me to the hospital. I called her, and she gave me detailed information on how to get to the hospital. I then called directory assistance for Allen AME church in Tacoma. I would call this church and alert this pastor of our emergent situation. He was in a meeting, but would have his secretary call other pastors telling them to come to the hospital. He would be on his way later that evening.

I arrived at Harbor View Medical Center, stepped up to the counter and in what I considered to be a calm, professional voice, told them why I was there. My husband was being airlifted to this hospital. His name is Leander Coates. I don't know what is wrong with him. I know it must be pretty serious because they are bringing him here by helicopter. He is being brought in from Kent, Washington. Is he here yet? I was told the helicopter hadn't arrived yet but I could go to the waiting room and they would let me know when he arrived.

As I turned to leave the counter I saw familiar faces. Brett and Robin, neighbors who lived next door to the church greeted me and we went into the waiting room. Gene Harden, the member of my congregation who had dropped Phil off at home had called them. Phil had called Gene to come back and take him to the hospital because Phil wasn't allowed to ride in the helicopter with Leander and the medical team. It wasn't long before the waiting room of the hospital began filling up with ministers, pastors, and well-wishers.

Waiting. More waiting.

Before long I went back to the counter and was told that Leander had arrived but I wouldn't be allowed to see him yet because the doctors were working on him.

Waiting. More waiting.

Trying to be patient and not cause a scene, I sat quietly praying or stood and paced the floor. More people came. Phil finally came, and I tried to find out what happened from him. He really couldn't tell me; I think he was in shock. At this point, I was still thinking Leander must have had another heart attack.

I gauged my response by the memory of Leander's previous heart attack. I'll never forget that morning. He woke me up at two o'clock and said, "Honey, my arm is hurting." This was the only symptom he divulged. Later I would hear of the nausea and upset stomach. Disoriented and not wanting to get up because of the time of morning, we rationalized that his discomfort was heartburn or gas. Maybe he'd eaten something that didn't agree with him. He seemed pretty uncomfortable so I told him this wasn't the time to be coy, he should belch or fart so he could feel better. At that moment, he clutched his arm and started sweating.

I grabbed his pants, gave them to him to put on, and grabbed my clothes to dress at the same time. I helped him to the car and got him from our bed to the hospital bed in seven minutes. I pulled up to the door of the emergency room, put the car in park, and ran inside exclaiming that my husband may be having a heart attack. An attendant in the emergency room rushed to the car with a wheelchair to get him. As I parked the car they began working on him. He was still alert, and when I came into his room they were drawing blood and some spilled on the floor. We laughed and said even when having a heart attack he would feed the vampires. The doctors determined he'd had a heart attack and began treating him immediately. I remember hearing those words as I stood at the door of his room in the emergency room. I then reeled around the wall so he wouldn't see me break down in tears.

That had been trauma before, but this was different.

They wouldn't let me see him. I wasn't feeling him. We had been very close. We did almost everything together. We held hands even when we were riding down the street in the car. We held hands while walking down the street, through the airport, in the grocery store or through the mall. We would think of each other at the same moment sometimes, and our phones would ring at the same time. But now I wasn't feeling him. From the time we met, we had bonded and enjoyed a kindred spirit. We were able to feel each other. We were able to speak to one another without an audible sound. It didn't take a lot of conversation between us because we had this thing going on that transcended words. Sometimes, if we tried to explain what we felt and how we were connected, words got in the way. But now, I wanted a word. Any word. Any feeling. Any sign telling me he was reaching out to me. I felt so empty, so helpless, and so alone.

I was finally going to be able to see him. One of the people visiting me had a friend who worked in the hospital. She explained to her friend that my husband was a minister and I was a minister and that they needed to let me see him. A few minutes later a nurse came to the door of the waiting room and told me I could see Leander. She apologized for the delay and again explained that the doctors were working on him. I walked those few feet through the buzzer-operated door and was guided down a hallway into a room where Leander was lying on a table. A male nurse came and led me toward Leander.

I took one look at him and was faced with the death of my husband. As I think back now, I can't remember whether or not he was breathing with the help of a respirator, but he must have been. He lay there so still, so lifeless. So unlike the vibrant, joyful man I loved. When I walked into a room where he was, he would say, "Hi, baby." There was no sound of his deep, melodious voice. The only sound I heard were those of voices coming from other areas, medical staff asking questions of patients and families and the rustling of curtains that separated the attending areas.

The doctor began to explain that Leander has had a brain bleed. "Is that an aneurysm?" I asked. No, a vessel in his brain has erupted. I asked the doctor, "Should I call his family?" He said gently, "Yes." The doctor looked at me as though he was reading my expression. He had such a kind face. I could tell he had been at this place with families before. It was also obvious that this was not easy for him. It wasn't easy for me either. I knew immediately that this was the beginning of a new journey toward the end of Leander's life.

The doctor explained a procedure they could try and asked if I would like him to perform a ventriculostomy. One common problem related to brain bleeding is hydrocephalus, which is the accumulation of a water-like fluid within the brain cavities, called ventricles. To solve this problem, the fluid may need to be drained with a special procedure called ventriculostomy. This procedure would be accomplished by drilling a small hole in his head to try and relieve some of the pressure building up in his brain. I said, "Yes. Do whatever you can to save my husband's life." He would be able to do this procedure in the ICU as soon as Leander was moved to the ICU unit.

Before leaving the room I called Leander's name. No response. I kissed him. No response. So I went back into the waiting room to wait for a response, and at this point I knew the next response would come from God. I called Leander's sister in Louisiana and told her to call everyone in the family to let them know they should come as soon as possible. I called my family in California and told them to pray. I felt as though I had been socked in the stomach and dared not say a word. It seemed as if my thoughts were in slow motion. Looking back, it felt like a moment from a Spike Lee movie when the world was passing by while I was hardly moving. Someone asked me if I was hungry. No. The hunger pangs of earlier that day had disappeared.

Phil and I decided to take a walk. We walked through the outer hallway of the hospital and talked. He asked me if I was OK. I really didn't know how I was, except I had this incredible feeling of peace. I shared with him that I felt Leander was gone, but I felt peace. Phil begged me to talk to the Lord and ask for more time. He wasn't ready. I wasn't ready either, but it seemed as if God had spoken. And for now all we could do was wait.

Waiting. More waiting.

We completed our walk and went back to the waiting room where the crowd continued to build. The nurse came and told us Leander had been taken to ICU and we could go to the waiting room in that area. This was great because there was a telephone, which allowed those who wanted to check in by phone to have a way of reaching us. There were about twelve of us there at the hospital, and I invited everyone to come into the ICU room to pray for Leander. The doctor was preparing to perform the ventriculostomy and I turned to him and asked him if he believed in God. He had a blank look on his face. I explained to him that I understood that it might not be politically correct to admit this publicly at his place of employment, but I assured him the only way he was going to perform this procedure on the man I loved was to let me know. He then said, "I believe." We all then gathered in a circle around Leander's bed to pray. I reached out my hand to the doctor and he took it. And we prayed.

Following the prayer we went back to the waiting room. As more people came and went we sat like zombies and continued "waiting." I would have been happy with any slight change in Leander's condition. Any movement. Any sound. This is one time that I would've been happy to have an uncomfortable conversation. I think I could've even shared a zydeco music moment with him. My husband was from Louisiana and loved zydeco music. I could take it or leave it. Mostly leave it, but I'd have shared it with him just to hear his deep, hearty, robust laugh. I'd have made him gumbo or dressing with oysters or a peach cobbler, anything to make him smile. People were coming and going, making conversation, but my mind was racing, trying to figure out what could have happened. A whirlwind of thoughts chasing each other, yet none of them coming to a complete conclusion.

The procedure was over and there was no change.

God Is Right!

I had a lump in my throat and a pain in the pit of my stomach. My appetite was gone. Water was the only substance I could handle. It was time to face reality. I needed my family, but they were too far away to comfort me. My parents and my sister live in Southern California. Although my daughter had moved back to Southern California a few weeks ago, it was now time to tell her to come back. I didn't want her to hear this tragic news through strangers. The news of Leander's hospitalization was traveling fast. She and Leander had the father-daughter relationship that was missing in the earlier stages of her life. The laughing, playing, fatherly advice, and strained conversations that dads have with their daughters were finally a part of her life and now it seemed this new-found relationship was coming to an abrupt halt. LaNicia and Leander hadn't parted on the best of terms, so I needed to get her back right away. I wanted her to get back and have the opportunity to clear things up with him. I didn't know the exact circumstances, but I was concerned that if he didn't survive this she would carry the burden of this unfinished business. The stress and strain of death is horrific enough on its own, but having unresolved issues combined with grief can have a very damaging emotional result.

I still hoped for a positive outcome, but the doctor's report and all the signs didn't look good. Upon our arrival in Washington, Leander began his job of presiding elder right away. Because of this position of leadership, people had heard of us but did not know us personally. This did not stop the outpouring of support. Many people were coming and going from the hospital waiting room at Harbor View Medical Center in Seattle. I had moved into the hospital waiting area just in case there was any change. The phone in the waiting room was constantly ringing from family members, pastors, and others from churches all across the United States.

As we sat in the waiting room with our many visitors, the doctors would occasionally come in to give me updates. Things didn't look good. There was no improvement. We were not alone when these updates came, and I would share these results with those surrounding us. Then the inquisitive questions began. What was I going to do? How did things look? What were the doctors saying? After many questions and many answers, I remember taking a pad and writing across the pad: *God is right*. And whenever the questions would come, I would just hold up the pad that said *God is right*. I didn't know how God was going to move, but I was convinced that however God moved, God was right!

How do we hold on to our faith when our hands and knees are shaking? How do we keep praising God when the outcome of our hopes seem dark? I learned from this experience that crying and feeling sad doesn't mean you don't have faith. It just means that you love someone enough to feel sad because of his or her condition. The doctors were not giving us any good news. They were running routine tests, as well as brain scans and EKGs. Leander's vital signs were actually good, but he had no brain activity. We were holding on to hope beyond hope. We knew God would intervene, yet I had talked with our family, and we knew that the time was coming that we would have to make a very hard decision.

We wanted to do everything we could do to let Leander know we were there. We brought a CD player into Leander's room and played music. He loved hearing me sing and I have been blessed to have two musical CDs, *Grateful* and *It's Christmas. Rejoice!* So we began playing my music and music from other artists. We sang along, hoping he'd hear our voices and join in. We held his hand, touched his head, talked to him, read the Bible to him, and still there was no response. I thought at one time there was some activity. I felt him squeeze my hand. That gave us hope. But, we later were told he was having seizures. Because I wanted the nurses and doctors to see him alive, I brought in pictures of the two of us and taped them on the window, along with cards and other sayings that would encourage him (if he woke up) and the medical team as they ministered healing to him.

Leander developed pneumonia and began running a very high fever. Almost simultaneously, his bowels began to release. The smell was horrendous. This made it difficult for us to stay with him for long periods of time. The nurses opened the windows nearest his bed and brought in a powerful electric fan to help reduce his fever and the stench that had developed. This was in December and the days and nights were chilly. It was also raining, and the damp air drove in a chill through the open window. So the chill coupled with the smell drove us out of his room. Periodically, we would bundle up and come back in to look at his lifeless body that was now being rotated in a mechanical bed. Still no change in his condition.

During this whole season of waiting on God's next move, Phil, LaNicia and I took up residence in the waiting room at Harbor View Medical Center. There were only a few occasions when we'd go home to take a shower, grab some clothes, and come back. On a Saturday night I left around midnight to go home, take a nap, dress for church and come back to the hospital. That Sunday morning I wore one of Leander's favorite outfits and came by the hospital to let him know I was on my way to church to preach about God's peace. After giving him a mini-lesson on peace and promising my quick return, I kissed him and went to church. Phil, LaNicia and I returned a few hours later, hung a blanket over the waiting room window, changed clothes, and we assumed our waiting room takeover position. We made frequent trips to his area in ICU to talk to him and let him know we were there. And my stay continued through early Thursday morning.

The days began to run together. It wasn't long before I didn't know what day it was. We were catching small naps on very uncomfortable chairs. The chairs were three or four individual armchairs fused together. We either had to lift our legs over the arms or find a way to get a leg through the arch of the arm to lie straight. The only one able to do the latter was Phil because he weighed less. But we weren't looking for comfort, we were looking for life. Any sign of life that would tell us Leander was going to be all right. I would've been fine with a hospital stay for him. We would just bring him pajamas, a toothbrush, a brush, and a Bible. That would be enough for him. Then we would go and come during normal visiting hours. Maybe I'd stay overnight sometime since I had difficulty sleeping without him. We had experienced this during the times that one of us would be out of town. We'd end up calling each other and talking on the phone until we could fall asleep. Only to wake up early the next morning needing to hear each other's voice again. I would have done anything just to hear his voice.

We had meetings with the medical staff. By now his two brothers, one from Houston, the other from Baton Rouge, had arrived and were brought up to speed on his condition and what the prognosis was. We all knew he didn't want to be on life support, although I knew by now that life support was artificially keeping him alive. The doctors told us no brain activity was recorded on the brain scan. His vitals were still working, but there was no brain activity.

The last meeting with the hospital staff was scheduled for Wednesday afternoon, December 5, 2001. The family was asked to come into a conference room and make a decision. The doctors and technicians had taken me to see the x-ray of Leander's brain. His brain had a gaping hole in it that they were unable to close. And now it was time to have a meeting to discuss the quality of life that remained for Leander and our opportunity to make the best decision for him. We were told that the machines were keeping Leander alive. There was nothing else they could do. They told us he would never have a quality of life anymore because his brain's function had ceased. We could leave him connected to the machines, and he would remain in this vegetative state for years, or we could make the decision to release him and allow him to die with some dignity intact. We asked several questions. What about the movement? The answer was he was having seizures. Were they sure there was nothing else they could do? They were sure. If we chose to turn the machines off, how long would it be before he was gone? They predicted a matter of minutes. I gave the go-ahead to release him from the machines. They would start a morphine drip, and God would do the rest in His own time.

Clinging to my faith, I knew whatever God chose for the outcome of this tragic occurrence was in His hands. Romans 8:28 says "And we know that all things work together for good to those who love God, to those who are the called according to His purpose." I love the Lord, but how could Leander's death be for my good? I didn't know then and still don't know. I've tried to understand God's way of doing things and I've searched for an answer or a clue. I don't know, maybe I loved Leander too much. Maybe I honored him too much. Maybe I appreciated him too much. I don't know. All I know is I trust God. And however God brings us out of this situation I will continue to trust God because *God is right.*

CHAPTER 3

Rainy Days and Thursdays

On Wednesday evening around seven o'clock the life support machines were released from their function to keep Leander alive. We released Leander to go home and be with the Lord. The doctors expected him to go quickly, but they didn't know Leander like we did. He was stubborn and would go when he was ready. The nurse began a morphine drip to lessen the intensity of his passing. We stayed by his bedside watching, waiting, and praying. Those who had held this vigil with us began going home or to check on others who were in other hospitals nearby. Nine-and-a-half hours after being removed from life support, on Thursday, December 6, 2001 at 4:28 AM, Leander took his last breath. For a while I wondered if maybe Leander were going to stay with us after all. The doctors had expected him to go quickly. We had said our goodbyes. It wasn't our usual goodbye because there was no response or movement from him. There was a moment around eleven o'clock that night when he let out a pretty ugly growl that startled all of us. In fact Phil said, "Man, I'm gonna go and let you have your privacy." Then Phil went back into the waiting room.

Thursday became a difficult day for me. It didn't matter what week it was in, I had difficulty on Thursdays. Leander had the brain bleed on a Thursday. He died on a Thursday, and his funeral was on a Thursday. Just a few weeks earlier, Thursday had become a day that

I would describe as the day of death. Thursday, November 15, a dear sister, Rev. Sylvia Drew, passed away in Kansas City, Missouri. The next Thursday, November 22, Thanksgiving Day, a dear brother, Rev. O. C. Smith, passed away in Los Angeles. The next Thursday, November 29, Leander had a brain bleed. The next Thursday, December 6, he went home to be with the Lord. The next Thursday, December 13, was the first of his three homegoing celebrations.

On Thursday morning, December 6, 2001 we were still waiting by Leander's bedside. The process of dying was taking longer than all of us had expected. Around 3 AM one of his brothers asked me to take him to pack and then to the airport since he had a 6 AM flight to catch. He knew Leander was dying, and he wanted to go home and prepare to perhaps come back for the memorial service. I thought this seemed to be a good plan because it looked as if Leander might be with us for the rest of the day. I'd run this errand and come back to wait for any changes. Leander's younger brother would stay at the hospital and call us if there was any change while we were gone. So we left the hospital at 3:45 AM. We had about a 35-minute ride to the house. I decided that while Leander's brother packed, I'd let my head hit the pillow in my own bed. Just as I lay down, the phone rang. It was Leander's youngest brother. Leander was gone. It was as if Leander didn't want us to see him take his last breath because almost as soon as we left, he left too.

I remember the rain splashing on the windshield of the car as we left the hospital for the drive to our house that morning. I had to drive slower than 60 MPH because the speed limit of 60 MPH is for driving in normal conditions and on dry roads. Every now and then we would hit a puddle of water and see it splash, or a vehicle would pass by us and cause a stream of water to cover the car. After we arrived at the house I could hear the raindrops and then the downpour of rain. But after we got the phone call that Leander's passage was complete, the rain stopped. I didn't see rain again until the next Thursday. Thursday became a day to remember, a day to mourn, a difficult day, and a rainy day.

The next Thursday we would have the first of three funeral/memorial services honoring Leander's life. The next few days became very hazy. There was the overwhelming amount of activity. The preparations for memorial tributes in three cities, arrangements, travel, and so forth had to be made. The phone calls had begun the week before, after the news spread that Leander was in the hospital and the outcome didn't look good. The calls were coming in from everywhere. My family in California, and his family in Texas, Utah, and Louisiana. The phones were constantly ringing. Friends and extended family from all over the United States called, expressing their love and concern. The phones were constantly ringing. The calls increased after everyone realized he had died. All of the phones we had were constantly ringing. The house phone, both of our cell phones, the kids' cell phones, and the church office phones, where someone was posted to answer them. I honored his life with three services. One in Seattle, Washington; one in Baton Rouge, Louisiana (where I would bury him); and a memorial service in Omaha, Nebraska.

The first service was in Seattle. Seattle, known for its rain, did not disappoint all the family and friends who came to say farewell to Leander and lend their support to Phil, LaNicia, and me. The rain began early in the morning the day of the funeral in Seattle. We woke up that morning to the pitter-patter of splashing as the raindrops included themselves in this ceremonial exit. The effect of early morning rain has always lulled my body into the embrace of sleep. Rainy days are the kinds of days that make you want to sleep in or turn up the heat and curl up with a good book. But this was not the case for me that day.

For a while after Leander died, I woke up every morning at the time of his death—4:28 AM. And this Thursday was no exception. I wondered if this occurrence would ever end. Waking so early and not getting enough sleep was beginning to take its toll on me. I wasn't falling asleep until after midnight, and then I'd wake up like clockwork at 4:28 AM. This day, I got up and began preparing for a day I was dreading. I would take a shower, relax, read the Bible, and wait for a volunteer makeup artist to arrive. She and others began arriving around eight o'clock. A friend, a pastor, my family, all began filling the house and preparing for this long, wet ride.

The family car arrived and we began passing out umbrellas and raincoats for the trip to the church. Most of the drive was a blur to me. But the real blur occurred when a car passed to the left of this limo and splashed a huge puddle of water over the top of the limo, forcing the driver to slam on his brakes. He couldn't see and the safest thing to do was stop the car.

We arrived at the church, and as we walked there were people along the walkway toward the entrance of the church placing umbrellas over our heads until we got inside. A sea of faces braved the wet roads and highways to lend support to our family, and we are forever grateful. Even though most of that day and many days that followed are a blur, I do remember the hugs and the thoughtful words that were spoken by most who were in attendance. Many people came from all over the country. Bishops, presiding elders, pastors, ministers, missionaries, stewardesses (mother's of the church), choir members, and others we did not even know. The service was wonderful. We are grateful for the music, prayers, and excellent eulogy by Bishop John Richard Bryant, Presiding Prelate of the Fifth Episcopal District of the African Methodist Episcopal Church.

For a long time, I found myself counting the weeks since Leander's passing by counting Thursdays. But things have gotten a lot better. There are some Thursdays that come and go now without notice.

Thank God for Green Beans

My appetite left the premises on November 29, 2001. When I am stressed-out, the first thing to go is my appetite. The last time I'd thought of food up to the time of the funeral was when I was waiting on Leander to take me to lunch. I was hungry and getting grouchy waiting for him to arrive. But from the moment I called home and found out his condition, the last thing on my mind was food. Was I hungry? I don't know. I had lost the sense of being in touch with feelings of hunger. In fact, all my senses were dull. I think I temporarily lost *all* feelings. My taste buds had taken leave of their senses. While Leander was in the hospital, I remember several people bringing food, but when I tried to eat, my mouth was so dry the food tasted like straw or mud. I would drink water or fruit juices, but I had lost the desire to eat. It was as though eating was too hard, too toilsome, and too much effort. My thoughts at that time were to get Leander well and get him home. Soon after learning his condition, the smell of food was nauseating.

A couple of days after Leander passed away, one of the local ministers had a member of his church cook a lot of food and bring it over to our house. Everyone remarked about how good the food was. The house became a whirlwind of smells with the many different food preparations being dropped off. Our loved ones were bringing chicken and roasts, salads, desserts, and green beans. Lots of green beans! Thank God for green beans. Every few hours someone would prepare a plate of food for me trying to get me to eat something. They'd say, "You're going to get sick if you don't eat. Why don't you try and eat something?" So I'd pick at the food on the plate, but somehow the only food that tasted like anything to me was the green beans. As soon as the word got out that I would eat green beans, the kitchen soon became filled with green beans. Green beans cooked and well seasoned with no pork of any kind. I would eat green beans with turkey or poultry products only. So I quickly adapted to a diet of green beans and water.

I am the cook of our family. In fact, when I lived in Redondo Beach, California, family holiday dinners were at my house. I have always cooked for my children, providing them with well-balanced meals. Can you imagine what it is like when the cook has no appetite or energy to cook? Thank God for the many people who fed my family, my visitors and tried to supply nourishment for me. People tried everything. One person brought fresh bread, fresh cheeses, fruit, and sliced turkey. He told me it was just what I needed to be eating, that I shouldn't worry myself with cooking or eating heavy foods. He didn't know that I wasn't eating or cooking at all.

My clothes were fitting better. That's always a welcomed reality. But I had no energy. I didn't want to talk or eat. What I wanted wasn't possible. I wanted my husband, alive and bubbly. But that was beyond my control. I don't remember how it came about that I began eating green beans. God is so awesome. There are many times in our lives that unexplainable things happen and we know that they were guided by the hand of God. And this was one of them. There were many people coming to the house to bring food, offer help, and so on. One of the members of my congregation took charge of the kitchen. I believe the Lord sent her there to be certain I didn't die of starvation. She kept trying in different ways to get me to eat something. So it might've been her nudging that led me to try eating green beans. All I can remember is once I began eating green beans, the word went out, and green beans were being prepared and brought to my house.

Thanks God for green beans. They sustained my life and nourished my body as grief invaded my existence with a vengeance.

CHAPTER 4

Functioning but Not Feeling

WE MADE IT THROUGH the three memorial services and returned to our home in Kent. We were tired and weary from the travel, yet I tried to get back to work immediately. I am so glad that I write things down, things that I have to do. If it had not been for my Franklin planner (appointment book) and a list of things to do at the church, I might've been found standing in the middle of the street looking lost. I was going through the motions of daily life. I was following lists and directions because my mind just wasn't functioning.

This was quite unusual for me. I am always in control and always staying on top of things. Now I was losing items and forgetting things at an alarming rate. I would look for my keys only to realize they were in my hand. I lost my purse several times and would find it where I had just looked. Thank God for my kids. Thank God my daughter came home when Leander was in the hospital. She and Phil took me by the hand and guided me through some really tough days. They would say, "Eat," and I would eat. They would say, "Go to bed," and I would go to bed. That's the way it went for a while. I wasn't sleeping through the night. I was still waking up at 4:28 AM every morning for quite a while. I was fatigued. When I looked in the mirror, a strange face was looking back at me. There were times when I would stare at the eyes in the face in the mirror, searching for an answer. Searching for the space where I used to reside. I didn't know myself anymore. I didn't even recognize my own voice.

I can remember going through the house searching because I heard someone screaming. I felt so silly when I came to myself and realized I was the one who was screaming. I was sure I wasn't having a nervous breakdown, but the reality of my husband's death was too much to handle.

Immediately following his death, our family suffered from losing him and the physical reminders that confirmed his death. There were still signs of his struggle to hold on to life in our bedroom. There was a puddle of blood on the carpet where Leander had most likely lost consciousness in our bedroom. Initially, I just covered it up with towels. I'd get to it as soon as I could. I don't know why I thought I should clean it up, but that's what I thought. Gene Harden, an officer of our church who loves assisting pastors, volunteered to get the carpet cleaned. He brought a carpet cleaner over one morning to get the stain up. Phil let them in the house. And when they arrived I was sitting on the edge of my bathtub, in my pajamas, crying hysterically. I remember this gentleman coming into my bathroom, taking me by the arm, and leading me down the stairs so I wouldn't have to watch the carpet stain being removed. I can't believe I walked in front of two men in my pajamas! So many of my steps eluded me during the time immediately following Leander's death. I was going through the motions of life, doing what had to be done. I was still preaching, teaching, presiding over meetings, yet I was not feeling like myself at all.

Thank God I knew my job fairly well. The congregation I had just begun serving didn't know me well anyway. I was sure that my personality had been altered by my loss. I was a different person now than I had been two weeks, two months, or two years ago, but since they didn't know me well, they got to meet whoever I'd become because of my husband's death. I was trying really hard to remember who Gwendolyn was. How did I act before? What was my personality like? How did I react to life? When did I laugh? I really couldn't remember laughing. I would eke out a weak smile. But in private, I cried a lot. In public I became this efficient person who emerged to get the job done.

More Than Tears

I think I have exceeded the amount of tears allotted to any human being. Tears in the morning, tears at midday, and tears that well up in my eyes at the mention of his name. Tears because of memories of all the beautiful sunrises and sunsets that we shared. Tears intertwined with laughter. Tears in the midnight hours staining the pillowcase. And just when I think the tears have ended, more tears.

You can see the tears, but you can't see the heartache. You can't see the pain lurking inside my body looking for a place to reside. The pain of this sudden occurrence has blown me away. I can't believe it. I find myself talking to, reminding, and convincing myself that Leander is not coming back. He is not away on a business trip to return in a few days or weeks or months. Many days I have to tell myself to get up in the morning, brush my teeth, take a shower, get dressed, get breakfast, check my schedule, and keep moving. This pain is like an unwelcome growth that is uncomfortable and keeps growing.

Because I chose to hide my pain on the inside, it was not long before I paid the price physically. My blood pressure was reaching high and dangerous zones. Some days my body was in so much pain that everything hurt. There was no explanation for the pain; I just hurt all over. Some days I just felt guilty. Guilty because I went to work on November 29th. If I had been there, the turn of events would have been in our favor. Leander would still be alive. We'd still be very much in love, we would be experiencing the Pacific Northwest together, and we would have created new memories. Of course I know better. I'm not trying to play God, but maybe I could have done something. We'll never know what happened in those hours between my leaving home at approximately 9:30 AM and Phil finding him around 2:30 PM. What happened? I don't know. How long did he lie on the floor after collapsing? What were his last words? If we had found him earlier would he still be alive? I'll never know.

The psychosomatic trauma of the death of my husband has been overwhelming. Grief has caused me to reinvent my life, lifestyle, and habits. Grief is more than swollen nasal passages and red eyes caused by crying. This intense emotional suffering is caused by the death of the person closest to me in the whole world. The experts say the death of a spouse is the most traumatic loss a person experiences. I know that God sees my heartache and takes my loss seriously. I know that God is a God of comfort. I've ministered to my family and myself regarding Leander's death. I've quoted scriptures reminding us that God never puts more on us than we can bear. Yet, after the tears are no longer visible, I still feel as if there's a hole in my heart. I have quoted Romans 8:28: "And we know that all things work together for good to those who love God, to those who are the called according to His purpose." Why this scripture has continually come to mind I don't know. I know that I trust God and eventually God will show me how this is for my good.

It wasn't long after Leander's death that I was called upon to minister to others who were hurting from the loss of their spouses. But it never failed. When all the ministering was over, I still came face to face with my own reality. Recognizing my own loss and feeling my own pain, I realized this was deeper than tears. I had acute sorrow and deep sadness. Filling my life with activity has not been the solution. Activity had temporarily delayed my pain but my body was reacting to my improper treatment of the grief that surrounded my every move. There were many days when I could not make myself get out of bed. In fact there still are some days that grief grips me and I become immobilized. My blood pressure has soared to numbers I've never seen before. There has been no explanation for this except unresolved grief.

All of us have heard of the stages of grief. The stages of grief would suggest that those who grieve go through a process that is predictable. However research has proven that grieving is not so predictable. There is no normal pattern or timeline for grief. Whatever experience or feeling a grieving person goes through after the death of a loved one is within the norm.

Additionally, everyone is different. And everyone grieves in a different way. No one can predict how you will feel, act, or interact. I have done things that I am sure are a direct result of grief. I must admit that I have helped others who have been unprepared for death because of my own experience. "Blessed be the God and Father of our Lord Jesus Christ, the Father of mercies and God of all comfort, who comforts us in all our tribulation, that we may be able to comfort those who are in any trouble, with the comfort with which we ourselves are comforted by God." 2 Corinthians 1: 3-4. Our experience awakens us to the condition of others. It is true that you don't understand until it happens to you.

CHAPTER 5

Suddenly Single

I WASN'T READY FOR LEANDER TO DIE. That was what I said to the Lord when I heard the Lord's voice as I was leaving my office on November 29, 2001. Ready or not, I am now suddenly single. Without any warning or preparation I have now found myself to be suddenly single. This is different than being single by choice. I've been married before and this is the first time my marriage has ended in the death of my husband. My other marriages, or legal relationships as I prefer to call them, ended because of the death of the marriage. After filing for divorce and before the ink was dry on the divorce papers, I would be advertising myself as a single woman. But this is different. In fact, I don't want to be single. As a matter of fact I am not just single. I am a widow. I am suddenly single. Because of Leander's death my days as a couple have been cut short. I find it hard to cope with the fact that Leander is no longer alive.

I sympathize with all the families and spouses who have lost loved ones. I feel your pain. I understand the instant pain and grief felt when unexpected death enters your life. On September 11th, many families were suddenly wrenched apart. There are those who would try and qualify loss as though there is some formula to explain how to feel and/or react based on how the loss occurred and to whom. The tragedy of September 11th is a horrific way for someone to die and it is not to be compared, but loss is loss, tragedy is tragedy, and pain is pain. When we experience loss, sadness, and grief our brain doesn't try to figure out different formulas to express that sadness. Our brain doesn't compartmentalize our pain and assign tears to the tear ducts and pain in the heart based on whom is lost or what is lost. Our brain just registers loss.

We are never comfortable with or totally prepared for death, even though some deaths leave us more in a state of shock than others. When someone dies after a lengthy illness, this leads to awareness or the possibility of the person dying. Death is never easy on those left behind, but an illness somewhat prepares family and friends for the eventuality. But in my case, I left a man who was alive at home on that morning. The last thing on my mind was burying him two weeks later. My mind was focused on the wonderful life we would share together. In fact, our favorite saying was "Together forever." We purchased items such as artwork, cups, and cards to that effect. We talked about the things we'd like to do together later on in life. We didn't really want ever to retire. We felt that becoming a certain age shouldn't dictate what our activities should be. We both enjoyed ministry immensely, but we knew that after age seventy-five we would have to retire from pastoral ministry in the AME church. So we talked about organizing a nondenominational church after retirement and pastor it until God called us home. It is amazing how many dreams die when someone dies. It is also amazing how many dreams live on through the persons still alive.

Since the death of my husband, I feel led to share my story with others who have experienced a similar loss. I have established a ministry, Suddenly Single Ministries (www.suddenly-single.org) as a way to reach out to those who feel lonely and alone following the death of a spouse. We have extended it to divorcees who have their own type of grief. We try to appeal to those who are not bitter due to their loss.

Widow

How many of us have joked about being the Monday night widow when husbands are caught up in Monday night football? How many times have we felt like widows when washing dishes, shopping at the mall, or just waiting for him to come home—and sometimes he does, sometimes he doesn't? Well, this is quite different. The first time I realized I would now be referred to as a widow, it was a jolting realization. I'd just settled into being comfortable being referred to as married. I had been married, or what I refer to as legal relationships, before. But to me those relationships were just that—legal relationships. I never changed my name, my bank account, or my marital status during those times. My maiden name is Phillips, and my previous spouses were sometimes referred to as Mr. Phillips when we went places where I was known and they weren't. But this time was different. I was Leander's wife in every sense of the word. Name, bank account, and rib. I was his rib. Bone of his bone, flesh of his flesh. I finally understood what being one flesh meant. All too soon, I am now being called a widow.

As mentioned previously, we had three Homegoing celebrations for Leander in the cities of Seattle, Baton Rouge, and Omaha. While traveling from Baton Rouge to Omaha, my daughter suggested we get a mileage program card for the airline we were traveling on. We were at the airport quite early for our flight for two reasons. For one thing, Leander died just a few months after September 11, and security procedures at the airlines had changed. Passengers were required to arrive at least two hours' prior to taking a flight. Also, we were leaving Leander's burial in Baton Rouge, his birthplace and where his family lives, and because we had not planned to stay long after the burial my children and I headed out to the airport even earlier than required. We had a lot of extra time on our hands and that's when we decided to enroll in the mileage plan of this airline. Everything went just fine until the person enrolling us asked my marital status. It was at that moment that I had to come to grips with the fact that I was now a widow.

I no longer have a husband to hold my hand. I no longer have a husband to kiss good night or good morning. My feet are now cold because there is no warm body to warm them. I am not ready for this. This is not on my agenda. This was not my plan. I wanted to grow old with him, not outlive him. I wanted more time. We had talked about so many things we wanted to do. He wanted to one day move back to Louisiana and build a house with a little church on the same property. I don't like Louisiana, but I loved him as I still love him and would have moved there just to make him happy. We loved traveling and wanted to take many trips to sunny places and bask in the sun. We loved exploring new areas. And we looked forward to experiencing the Pacific Northwest together.

And now, I am a widow. I have no experience. I don't know the proper etiquette. I fumbled over the word for a long time. Marital Status? Um,.um . . . widow. Widow. What comes to your mind when you hear the word widow? Of course, I know that it is the honored title bestowed upon women whose husbands have died. But I had never given the word much thought before becoming one. Since becoming a widow, I have observed people when they are told I am a widow. This information sometimes evokes a sad countenance and other times an exclamation of unbelief. In fact, there are some who have entered widowhood who do not, cannot, and will not bring themselves to accept the title widow. This is for many reasons, including 1.) Denial—accepting this title is to accept the death of her husband; 2.) Vanity—being a widow is thought to be a distinction for old women; and 3.) There's no love lost—there are some spouses who didn't love their spouses and are glad they're gone.

I am blessed to have had the experience of being married to Leander. I had been married before, but I finally got it right with Leander. He knew how to treat a lady. He loved giving me red or yellow roses. He opened the car door for me, complimented me every day as though it were our first date, supported me in my creative and spiritual work, and loved me unconditionally. He made me blush and feel like a schoolgirl all the time. There were several occasions in our courtship and marriage when he would bring roses to my job. He would hide behind the flowers (as if that were possible) and get the biggest kick out of the reaction of my coworkers. When I worked for a Catholic non-profit organization the majority of my coworkers were nuns. Leander really got a kick out of their interest in admiring and smelling the roses. Even though this gift of fresh, fragrant roses was his special love gift to me, each time I received them from him was like the first time. I never knew the day they would arrive, but I always knew they were on the way.

Leander and I had only been married a short time when he died. Even though it seemed like a long time, we had less than three years together as partners in life and ministry. When people saw us together, they assumed we had been married for over twenty-five years. I guess that was the Lord's way of providing a comfortable relationship that in earth years would be short, but by eternal standards the months counted as years. We even had anniversary cards to verify the eternal standard. When Leander and I decided to get married, the first date we chose didn't work out for us. We looked at the calendar for the next possible date, but my calendar was somewhat full. I was scheduled to leave for Senegal, West Africa, to perform in a musical concert with a 200-voice Senegalese choir later that month.

I came up with the brilliant idea that he could come with me to Senegal; we could get married there, and then get married again in the United States. So we did. After arriving in Senegal I was whisked away to perform and participate in a media blitz prior to the concert. Because this was my sixth trip to Senegal (Leander's first) and I had performed there on previous trips, I was pretty well known. It was announced on the radio that Leander and I would be getting married on a Wednesday night, and we were both amazed when over 1,000 people showed up for the ceremony.

Nineteen days later we married stateside in Pomona, California, with a much smaller crowd in attendance. On our first anniversary we began celebrating on the date of our first ceremony and gave each other a card and gift for each day between the two dates. I didn't know then how meaningful this would be. We just thought it was something cute and unique. But after Leander passed away and I opened a box that contained twenty-one anniversary cards, I understood that this was God's way of giving us the years without the benefit of actually spending this time as husband and wife. When I found that box I sat in the middle of the floor reading each one and remembering.

I Miss You

My days and nights are surrounded by sadness, loneliness, and grief. The days of Gwendolyn and Leander—the Couple—are gone and in the past. Living with only the memory of Leander is difficult. Each day creates a new set of circumstances, distractions, and joys. Because we were in ministry together, I still attend many of the events we attended together, and it is so interesting to see programs that he was so much a part of continue without the mention of his name. But I still miss Leander dearly. If it were possible to have a conversation with him right now, there are several things I'd tell him. So please indulge me as you have a front row seat to a conversation that I'll never get to say to him face to face, in this world anyway.

> Leander: My love, my darling,
>
> *I miss you. I miss our love. I miss your smile, your laughter, and your sweet embrace. I miss the way you always treat me like a lady. I miss your careful concern for our family and me. I want you to know how sorry I am for all the times that we didn't get along. I apologize for every word that I ever said to you that was harsh. I'd trade those words for whispering*

sweet nothings in your ear if I could. I would give anything to be in your arms for just one more night. I know you are in a better place, but I still miss you. No one can say "I love you" like you do. I miss your voice and the way you move me. I miss the walks in the park, the picnics, and the parades. It's been hard to sleep since you've been gone. You know I always have trouble sleeping when I'm not in your arms. I still remember the theme for our love and our wedding: Together Forever. Our love is etched in my heart for eternity.

Since you've been gone, a lot of things have happened. La-Nicia came back home. She now has her own apartment and a new sports car. She even sings occasionally at the church. Phil almost flunked out, but graduated from high school with his class. He really had a rough time keeping his head together because six weeks after you went to heaven, Ernest (Phil's biological father) died too. Phil took losing both of you pretty hard and had a few bumps after that. But, you'd really be proud of him now. He's turned his life around, accepted his call into the ministry, just received his AA degree and is continuing on toward a B A degree. He's also the youth pastor at the church and has released his first Holy Hip Hop Rap CD, The Responsibility That Comes with the Gift. His rap name is Sharpskills. And his skills are sharp.

Mom and Dad are just fine. No one believes he's eighty-six and she's eighty-five. Hope I have those genes. Bobby is home. He and Michella are doing well. We have a grandson, Mikkel. He was born on my birthday and for his first birthday I gave him a gift we'll all remember. I baptized him. If only you could have been there. It was the most awesome experience. Gloria and Tommy are having a great life. She has written a book Too Broken to Be Fixed, and their church and newspaper are doing great. We have a new nephew too. Steve has a son; you met his daughter. Steve has many recording projects too.

Goes by the name S.P. A lot of changes have taken place in the world and in our lives since you've been gone. Randy, Wayne, Charlie, and the rest of the family miss you too. Family gatherings just aren't the same without you.

I'm still the pastor at Walker Chapel and we're still working on building a great church with loving and caring people. I often wonder what things would've been like if you were still here leading the Pacific Northwest Conference.

Please know that we did everything we could to keep you alive. I'm so sorry I wasn't there with you that day. You know I would've done whatever I could to help you. It was out of our hands. And while we love you so much, God loves you more. And I'm not fighting with God. Hardly a day goes by that we don't mention your name. There are many times when we are having conversation, we add in a comment or two from you. Because we know exactly what you would've said. I still haven't learned to live without you. I just take it one day at a time. I am so glad that you were a part of my life. I am eternally grateful to God for that wonderful gift. And I will treasure your memory forever.

Loving and missing you,
Your baby, Gwendolyn

PART 2

THE PATH TO JOY

※

*We either make ourselves miserable
or we make ourselves strong.
The amount of work is the same.*

—Don Juan, *Journey to Ixtlan*

CHAPTER 6

Permission to Mourn

GRIEVING IS UNCOMFORTABLE. While it is natural, it is unusual. Although death occurs every day, it isn't every day that someone you love or someone who is close to you dies.

Death is unpredictable. You cannot grow accustomed to something that is unpredictable. Therefore, response to our grief is unpredictable. If you find yourself waking up in the morning having to talk to yourself or chart the steps you will take to make it through another day, it's OK. Many days and nights I have been disoriented, confused, and stuck in my sadness. I have been so paralyzed with grief that I felt bionic. Everything around me seemed unreal. I had to choose my steps carefully—one day at a time. The shock, terror and pain associated with grief can cause feelings of instability. I have moved through days, months, weeks, and now years since my husband's death, managing to do what was expected of me, yet I feel as though my body has participated but my mind was trapped in a fog. I knew my job and responsibilities so my automatic life-pilot system activated and proceeded through the days.

I didn't use wisdom, which would have encouraged me to take time off and get through this horrifying period in my life. I handled this experience in my normal way—I drowned it out with activity. Following Leander's death, I didn't take time to recover. In fact, I increased my workload, and my routine became more rigorous. Working longer hours, accepting more preaching, singing, and seminar engagements to keep busy. But at the end of the day, grief was always sitting at the door waiting for my arrival. I challenged my personal level of comfort by going to movies, dining out, and traveling *alone*. I was so good at maintaining the appearance of being OK that no one noticed or seemed to be concerned that I could be masking deep pain. I am sure this was based on my feeling that I needed to make others feel comfortable with my loss.

But my little charade came tumbling down in the form of illness in my body. I began experiencing muscle spasms and back problems on a regular basis. There were days when I literally could not get out of bed because of aches and pains. These symptoms were without any medical explanation. My blood pressure soared out of control, and I was packing on the pounds at an alarming rate even while eating less. Sleep became a luxury that I really appreciated because I didn't experience it often. I soon realized *I was having a problem*.

On one of many trips for medical attention, my doctor voiced his concern. Dr. Carlson leaned back in his chair, folded his arms, took off his glasses, looked me squarely in the face, and asked, "What's really going on?" He began to briefly discuss my medical record and his concern over my frequent visits. At that moment he became my therapist. He listened as I told him my story of sudden loss, which had capped a whole series of stressful events—the new job as pastor of a church in Washington, moving to a new location, being separated from family and close friendships by distance, needing to re-energize a hurting congregation, and so forth. All of these are major stressors. Stress has been described as the number one health problem in America. No wonder my body was reacting abnormally. At the end of sharing my "blues" with him, I quickly switched gears to tell of all the accomplishments, tasks, and projects (including school) that I had recently added to my plate.

By the time I finished unloading, I heard myself explaining a broken person chasing an overwhelming schedule. With one look at my doctor's face I could tell that he was summing up my case and coming to a conclusion. He said to me, "You're experiencing grief and you probably need to talk to somebody." He asked when I had last taken a vacation. He further suggested that I take a vacation, maybe find a boyfriend (I really wasn't ready to go there!), reduce my workload, talk to somebody, and take time to grieve. Before that conversation, I had never attributed any of my illness, lack of energy, insomnia, or overcrowded schedule to *grief.*

I have learned it for myself, and I pass this information on to you: grief is a normal reaction to loss. When we have loved someone and the loved one dies, it is impossible to get on with our lives until we have acknowledged that that person lived, meant something to us, and is now gone. The loss of a loved one is a stressful event. Sweeping this under a rug will just create a lump that will alter our lives. Our once smooth surface of life now has an uncomfortable bump to be dealt with. There is no right or wrong way to express grief. There is no time limit to begin or end the mourning of your loss. However, the sooner you grieve, the sooner you can heal. Don't let people, time, or circumstances determine how and when you react to your loss. In the midst of my grief, I had several well meaning, yet incorrect and misguided people interpreting my situation as though it were their own. I didn't know to guard my heart and my ears. I cannot even begin to retell all the foolish, unnecessary, and improper things people felt they had the right to say. This could be the time when people whose opinions you didn't respect before your loss want to become the expert on your life. No one knows or understands what you are going through other than you. Others may have had a similar loss but while losses are similar, reactions are individual. No one knows the dynamic that this death has had on your life.

After my husband died a woman came to me explaining that she knew exactly how I felt because her brother was ill. How can you compare the death of a spouse to the illness or even death of a brother? Both are real events and can have an effect on our lives, but there is a huge difference between the two events. I was so flabbergasted that I couldn't say a word. Thank God for a sister-friend of mine standing nearby who firmly corrected the misguided sympathy of this woman. If you have experienced the death of a loved one, I am sure you can bring to mind your own list of well meaning but stupid pieces of advice. This is a time of great vulnerability. Perhaps former grievers should become protectors of those new to grief. We all have our stories to tell.

Because my husband's death was unexpected, I had no time to plan or get help to deal with this tremendous loss. I've had people tell me to be sure and take time to mourn. What does that mean? It means different things to different people. I think I shied away from mourning and grieving because I misunderstood what that meant. I am not a total crybaby. My immediate concept of mourning was crying until my eyes were swollen and red, wearing black clothing for at least one year, not eating, looking sad, etc. But I discovered a healthier approach that has worked for me. And that approach is to *remember, write, and release.*

It took me a while after my doctor's visit to *really hear* what he had said. I would have to experience a few more episodes of illness, exhaustion, and other signs before I took time to care for myself and adopt a plan toward wellness. But eventually I made plans to go on a cruise to Alaska. I knew I needed to get away, take some time for myself, by myself, to face the issues in my life that were created and exacerbated by the death of my husband.

My choice of vacation spots had become clear during my discussions with three women; two female ministers and a layperson. We were in Albuquerque, New Mexico, at a Women's Prayer Conference. The convener of the conference, Rev. Cecelia Williams Bryant was hosting a luncheon for the participants of the conference in a lovely cottage in Old Town Albuquerque. Over lunch with these three new women acquaintances, we engaged in introductory talk and they soon became friends. Somehow our conversation moved to my need for a vacation. We laughed and talked while sharing our stories. The food and desserts were so good, and by the end of the meal we all agreed that a cruise was the most likely vacation to accomplish what I needed, grief work! Together we ruled out anyplace with access to landlines or cell phones since this was to be a time of reflection and healing. We also discussed that a cruise would present less distractions. In addition, if I didn't feel like going to the dining hall for dinner, I could order room service and it would be included in the cruise package price. On the other hand, if I felt like being around people, I would have that option. So it was settled in my mind and spirit.

I came back home and immediately made arrangements to go on a seven-day cruise to Alaska. I was to leave three weeks after returning from Albuquerque. I was clear on the assignment I would give myself. *Reflect, write and release.* This cruise was probably one of the best things I have ever done for myself. I began planning a trip that had the potential of moving me toward a fresh outlook on life. When packing, I would bring clothing and other essentials I thought would help me in this season of reflection: photos from our wedding, our trip to Africa, and our last vacation together, which had been a cruise to Mexico. I purchased a journal to capture feelings about my past, my pain, my present, and my future. And finally, I had a wonderful stateroom with a private balcony. This would be my place to release.

I had finally given myself permission to grieve. I did not know what to expect. So I prayed, asking the Lord for guidance, protection, and healing so when the path presented itself, I would not miss it.

Joy Comes In The Morning

> *Weeping endures for the night,*
> *but joy comes in the morning!*
>
> PSALM 30:5

It is true that *trouble don't last always*. Likewise the pain and suffering associated with grief will not last always. Joy will come in the morning. I don't know which morning will produce joy. It is different for everyone. I hope I have not signified an Alaskan cruise as a cure-all for grief. If this were the case, someone would have discovered this long before I did and would be making a *lot of money*. I can see the signs now: CRUISE FOR THE GRIEVING—GUARANTEED RESULTS. My experience from grief to joy is not a simple journey nor is it without work. It is not without a struggle, mental anguish, and fear. Uncharted waters always bring with them an element of fear. This journey of grief was my maiden voyage. I have neither experience nor frame of personal reference in the death of a husband. This is new to me. The loss of a loved one creates an unfamiliar space for us. Contrary to our belief that we might have said what we would do in certain circumstances, we do not know how we will act or react when loss occurs. Each experience of death and subsequent grief is different based on your relationship with the one who is now gone.

For nearly two years after Leander's death, I woke up every morning at 4:28 AM. It was as though a grief alarm had been implanted in my brain. During the day I felt totally drained. I tossed and turned during the night. My thoughts would unpack themselves at night following the busyness of my days. I cried most nights until sleep made a short visit. It would seem as though I had slept for long hours yet I would open my eyes and the clock would read 4:28 AM. This was a reminder of my loneliness and my loss. I felt I could talk to no one about this because everyone in my life expected me to model healthy and spiritual ways to cope and adjust to life's situations. I suffered in silence for over a year. Because I wasn't getting enough sleep or rest, I became very aware that *the night* can be long. I did everything short of taking prescription drugs to sleep at night. I didn't want to anesthetize or sedate myself. I just wanted to sleep. I tried over-the-counter valerian, Tylenol PM, and Sleepytime and chamomile tea. I tried staying up later only to experience more fatigue. I quoted Scriptures to myself, read the Bible and other books, prayed, and tried to concentrate on good thoughts, yet my heart was so captured by grief that sleep would not come. I was sad, lonely, and missing Leander. Everyone who has been through grief knows that the first year following the loss is the most difficult. It is called "going through the firsts." The first year without Leander was excruciatingly painful. The first Christmas, first birthday, first Easter, first Mother's Day, first Father's Day, first Annual Conference (AME Church) and first wedding anniversary alone drained me both physically and emotionally.

People kept telling me things would get better and easier—I just couldn't see how. I have always been a strong person, but this thing had gotten the best of me. My blood pressure was getting higher and higher. I was gaining weight without eating. My hair was falling out. I was constantly having back problems that would put me into bed for three to five days at a time. I was always agitated and irritable. I tried going to counseling, but the counselor was more intrigued with my life as a pastor, singer, writer, actor than helping me to resolve my issues. What was I going to do? I had no one to whom I felt comfortable sharing my true feelings. I kept preaching the Word of God and telling the congregation that God doesn't put more on us than we can bear, but somehow I was not getting the message I needed for myself. That was it! I was focusing on everybody and everything but myself, to the detriment of myself. What a concept!

I don't ever remember having a problem with joy. My personality is quite joyful. People like being around me because I am pleasant. I think positive. When Leander died, I did not feel like being happy.

I could not bring myself to smile and laugh. I chose to entertain myself by going to comedic movies, trying to find the strength to laugh. I did not feel like my old self. I knew I would never be the same again, but I just wanted the light to come back in my eyes.

I sometimes felt separated from reality and this was not pleasing to me so I spent time analyzing myself to figure out what my next moves should be. This meant I would spend time making sure Gwendolyn was healing, recuperating, and experiencing life to the fullest again. Even though it was hard for me to comprehend, I knew things would get better. After all, I felt things could not get any worse, so getting better should be an easy task. I had to remind myself of the many messages I'd shared with others on numerous occasions. I have always told people that joy is a choice. We can choose whether or not to have joy. I further explain that joy has nothing to do with circumstances. Joy does not depend on happiness nor does it change through sadness. It is a choice. Choose to stay in the painful emotions or work through them by choosing joy. God has given us the tools to help ourselves. If we want to feel better, we can. So I choose joy.

The cruise to Alaska was not the first trip I had taken since Leander's death. Because of my ministry, my own recovery was many times placed on extended hold while I met the needs of others. Some of these events were positive trade offs and proved to be learning experiences for me. Prior to going on my personal retreat, I was a workshop leader for a group of widows that traveled to Kingston, Jamaica. This excursion, led by Rev. Dr. Cecelia Williams Bryant, Episcopal Supervisor of the AME Fifth Episcopal District was themed *New Beginnings*. Widows in attendance were at varying stages of grief and recovery, ranging from five months to twenty-two years. I have learned from others who have survived the death of a husband. I was astonished to discover from our discussions that no recovery time limits can be placed on the surviving person after the death of a spouse. Imposed limits are for the comfort of those who are *not* grieving the loss. Some of us will never get over our losses. Other people in our lives may be ready for us to move on, but we cannot move on until *we* are ready. Grief does not have to keep us in its grip, but it takes the work of grieving to settle in the mind before moving on.

Women seem to have the most difficulty moving on. In ministering to widows, I am amazed at how graphic they are in the retelling of the events leading to the death of their husbands. The stories are told with clarity and passionate details as though they relive the experience with each retelling of it. One of the reasons I'm writing this book is to release my vivid memories to paper. It's still hard for me to tell my story without shedding tears. I remember each and every detail. But memories will not delay my reconnection with joy.

Joy does not come from people, nor is it activated by people. Joy is a gift from God. Unfortunately, some gifts are never opened or enjoyed by the recipients. Joy is a choice. Joy needs to be nurtured. Joy can be associated with but not limited to happiness. The root of happiness is joy. If there is no joy, happiness is impossible. Happiness without joy is false pretense. Have you ever seen people fake a smile and the only facial features involved in the smile are their lips and teeth? They have not engaged their facial muscles or their eyes, but their lips are curled and skinned back across their teeth. What a horrid sight. But when someone is indeed smiling—from the heart—it is a beautiful sight to behold. The entire face is engaged in this process. Fewer facial muscles are used for a real and sincere smile. A hearty smile is unmistakable. A smile from the heart, reaches the heart. Our faces reflect our true feelings. Check the expressions on people's faces and you can see who is joyful or really in pain. When you have joy, it bubbles up naturally from the inside of you and spills over to the outside without force. That's what I wanted to feel and exhibit again. My quest for joy took me to Norwegian Cruise Lines and off to Alaska.

I had to be intentional about the work I needed for myself. This cruise would be the perfect opportunity to do this work. I would not know anyone and would not have to keep up appearances. I had a room with a balcony all to myself. If I felt like screaming and crying I could open the balcony door and let it out. I packed a mini survival kit: a journal to capture my thoughts on paper, my Bible, and a novel (something lighthearted). My wardrobe would consist of cute and comfortable clothes, and plenty of sleep/lounge wear. I promised myself that I would be open-minded and not bring a bundle of preconceived ideas. I would pray and ask God's guidance as I embarked on my path to healing joy.

My daughter dropped me off at the pier the morning the cruise began. Her parting words instructed me not to tell people my occupation for fear they would dump their problems on me and prevent me from having the personal retreat I needed. After hugging me, she demanded I give her my cell phone, promising to call the ship if there was an emergency. I reluctantly conceded. I was really having trouble with myself. *I was abandoning my on-call, overworked, available lifestyle for seven days.* I knew I needed to go on this trip, and I also knew this was a life-changing opportunity. I would have to reprogram my mind to *take care of myself.* I was so used to taking care of everyone else, tending to the needs of others and definitely being reachable. Now, for seven days I would try to recapture and recover personal feelings and emotions. I would get in touch with my innermost thoughts, and God would guide me through this path for the next several days.

As a result of grief, I have discovered how easy it is to slip into depression and sadness. It is also difficult to recognize this and seek help. I had come to rely on family and friends to help snap me back into reality. Phone calls and visits by family and extended family helped me stay emotionally sound for a while. But the people who knew me best were many miles away. My parents and sister kept the lines of communication open for a while. Then we slipped back into our normal patterns of two to three contacts a week versus everyday.

I even had a couple of sistah-friends who came for a visit. Pat came for a few days before New Year's Day and Jackie came in June of the next year. In between those times I was miserable, but the people who loved me weren't close enough to see this and help bring me back. I promised myself that on the cruise I would confront these emotions and ask God to replace them with joy.

Looking back over this period in my life, I have come to realize that I was angry because of Leander's untimely demise. Since he wasn't around to receive my wrath, I reassigned the anger, with good cause, to those who gave cause for being the recipient. This quiet, unpronounced anger would be assigned to one of Leander's so-called friends. Leander was his friend but this man was certainly not a real friend to Leander. There was anger toward Leander's family members: his children, brothers, sisters, nieces, and nephews feeling their love and more communication might have kept him in better spirits while he was alive. This conclusion was legitimate because he loved them so much and felt detached from them by distance and attitudes.

I also had anger toward the church Leander loved. He loved the African Methodist Episcopal Church. His parents raised their children Catholic and African Methodist Episcopal. Out of this family came a Jesuit Priest and an AME pastor. I could not understand how a church group he loved so much could remove his name and the mention of his name from everything so soon. After six or seven months, it was as though he'd never had any role in the church, or even as if he'd never existed at all. Then, the beneficiary snafu regarding his life insurance with the church didn't help matters. Leander had been married previously and although we had sent in new forms, the changes he made to his policy with the church went overlooked. This was brought to the attention of the directors of the fund, but I didn't receive what was due me even after all the proper documentation was presented to the Employee Security Department. Our bishop called this department and I called a few times, but never received an answer or a return call. Because of this situation I advise everyone to look at all insurance policies, bank accounts, automobile loans, and medical records. Be certain the correct name is in all the appropriate places as beneficiary, next of kin, power of attorney, and so forth. This will eliminate some anger, added grief, or delayed grief due to lack of information or the inability to perform necessary functions. I had to rely on the opinion of someone I didn't respect or trust to make some final decisions as they related to my husband because I didn't have some needed information.

So, my joy was hiding beneath a lot of garbage. And since no one knew the load I was carrying, no one could release me from the bondage and baggage but me. I had to unpack and unload all of this garbage somewhere. The cruise to Alaska was going to be the dumping place for me. I decided to bundle up all my fears, feelings, anger, and emotions and release them during this week of regrouping. Yes, I was angry, but I was also grateful. Grateful for the many family members, friends, extended family, pastors, ministers, congregations, presiding elders, and bishops who loved us and assisted us during the most extreme time in my life. I knew I needed to have a frank discussion with myself. I wasn't sure if I needed to have discussions with anyone else, but I was prayerfully asking God to reveal to me what I should do. I was determined to come back from the cruise a changed woman, set free from everything that would steal, diminish, or kill my joy. I really had high hopes and great expectations considering this was a one-week cruise. I knew that I might not complete the work but I had faith that I would make great progress. At the writing of this book, I must say that I did make great strides and I am still progressing. One of the valuable lessons I will pass on is do not harbor feelings of anger. Harboring anger will kill your spirit. Anger was changing my attitude and personality. So to cleanse my thoughts and renew my spirit, I chose to have a personal, private, forgiveness ceremony. Forgiveness is powerful. It is powerful whether the party being forgiven knows they have been forgiven or not. There are a lot of people I have chosen to forgive. Some know it and some do not, and some will know it by my attitude if I am ever in their presence again. I am sure these people are not interested in whether or not they had any effect on me, but it is important that I know. I went out on the balcony of my room and spoke the names of those I would forgive to the wind, releasing them from my jail of anger.

Seven days is a long time to spend alone. Most of us don't spend a lot of quality time alone. I think we should. This experience has proven to be the best medicine for me. I kept the promise I made to myself to focus on my purpose and goal. It would have been easy to become absorbed with the activity on the ship and miss the opportunity and blessing of evaluating my state of being. I learned a lot about myself on that trip. Other than the fact that I did it, going alone, I learned that it is valuable from time to time to evaluate oneself. Additionally, I am learning to release those things that negatively affect me. I am keeping track of the good things in my life, and I thank God every day for my family, extended family, and friends. God has blessed my family and me so much these past few years. We have grown closer and more in love with one another.

If you have lost a spouse, here are some steps to helped you recover and embrace God's gift of life:

1) **Take time for yourself.** Give yourself time to heal. Rediscover who you are. Love yourself!

2) **Face reality.** Realize an enormous change has taken place in your life. Denial creates inner turmoil.

3) **Remember.** Find and/or create ways to honor the memory of your deceased loved one. There are many books written to help you on this journey. One that has been helpful to me is *A Passage Through Grief,* Barbara Baumgardner.

4) **Bitterness check.** If you are harboring any bitterness toward your loved one or anyone else—let it go.

5) **Forgive.** Forgive anyone and everyone who has ever hurt

or harmed you in any way, including your deceased loved one. Write a letter, talk to a picture, go to the grave and say the words. Have a personal and private forgiveness ceremony. Write on a piece of paper the names of those you wish to forgive, even your own name, then find a safe place to burn the list and discard the ashes. Holding on to the list would be the same as harboring the feeling of unforgiveness.

6) **Cry.** It's OK to cry. Have a good cry, and then have a good rest.

7) **Write.** Get a journal and write your feelings. Write your desires. Write your plan. Write your pain. Keep writing, and who knows you might have a best seller!

8) **Reach out.** Many times we withdraw when we are in pain. Deep inside we want people to notice and come rescue us. Newsflash! They don't. Participate in your rescue by asking for help. Be transparent. Be vulnerable. You'll never know what works until you try.

9) **Be supportive.** Thinking about others always makes us feel better. Reach out to others who are experiencing what you have experienced. Be a source of support and encouragement. When your focus is not always on yourself, you will reap positive benefits.

10) **Walk by faith.** This may be last on the list, but the last should really be first. This is the time to lean on the Lord. If you don't have a relationship with the Lord, this is the time to get one. See chapter 8 to find out how.

Discovering a New Normal

The cruise to Alaska proved to be a wonderful place to come to grips with my new life journey. This was the first time I'd gone on a week long vacation *alone*. I surprised myself when I actually followed through with a plan that was just for me. The pattern of my life has been consumed with work and providing for others. I have been a parent my entire adult life. Mostly, I have been a single parent with an ongoing need to provide food, clothing, and shelter for my children. At the time of Leander's death, Phil was sixteen and still required parental care. Most parents can relate to being consumed with the priority of rearing a family. I allocated most of my time off and vacations to be spent with my family, although I had occasionally taken a day or two by myself to relax in a nearby scenic area such as Palm Springs, San Diego or San Francisco.

My children were old enough to take care of themselves so I knew they would be fine as I took some time out for myself. This was a welcomed and timely adjustment, and frankly I was astonished that I had the sense to provide something so meaningful for myself. This was not a normal pattern in my life, but it is becoming a healthy new pattern, an acceptable life adjustment. My normal lifestyle as I knew it was shaken, so now my life is taking new form. I am being reshaped in my thinking and comfort level, and I enthusiastically participate in so many new things, such as going alone to restaurants, movies, concerts, and other events.

A year before taking the cruise, I ventured alone to Victoria, B.C. for four days. While the trip to Victoria was so close to Seattle it seemed far away because I was in another country. I was surprised on the trip to Victoria when halfway across the water my cell phone connection was lost. I didn't panic and was rather amused by this. I discovered that I was OK being out of touch with everyone for a few days. This helped me find the courage to continue the exploration of discovering a new normal and to accept new patterns as they emerge in my life.

The cruise to Alaska would prove to be the most effective self-awareness time of my life. While boarding the ship I was immediately reminded that I was alone. I observed that most other passengers traveled as couples, groups, or families. We left Seattle on Saturday afternoon. On Sunday we cruised the inside passages. Monday through Wednesday we visited Ketchikan, Juneau, and Skagway, Alaska. Thursday we visited Prince Rupert, British Columbia, before arriving back in Seattle on Saturday morning.

After boarding and having my picture taken, I made an appointment for a massage. I also made dinner reservations at one of the eight restaurants aboard. The ship offered eight dining choices outside of the main dining included in my package price. I didn't mind that there was a surcharge because I wanted to reward myself with a personal celebration for being so brave. My choice, Shogun Asian Restaurant was actually three dining experiences in one. Shogun features a teppanyaki room, sushi bar, and sit-down Asian fusion restaurant. I selected the teppanyaki room. This style of restaurant, similar to Beni Hana's, is where customers sit around a table for eight and the food is prepared on a center grill by an entertaining chef. This was also memorable because it was a type of restaurant Leander and I had enjoyed going to. On the other hand, this style of dining was particularly challenging because most other guests would be with spouse, family, or friends.

While waiting for my reservation time to enter the restaurant I met two friendly Mormon couples vacationing together. A bit nosily, they inquired if I was waiting for someone. When I told them no, I was a widow traveling alone, they were intrigued and we engaged in conversation. They found it fascinating that I was nervy enough to take a vacation alone and quickly adopted me. I tried diverting the conversation to other subjects but I had opened the door and their curious questions flooded in. Once seated at our table, I asked if they wouldn't mind talking about other things, allowing us to have a pleasant dinner. They agreed. After dinner, one of the wives, Jeanne, asked if she could call me another evening during the trip to see if I would meet them for dinner. I agreed. One of the husbands was a former bishop in the Mormon Church, and they were quite interesting. We've even spoken a few times since the trip.

After dinner that night we went together to the Karaoke Club. Not being able to resist participating and with a little coaxing from my newfound friends, I signed up to sing. After singing "The Greatest Love of All," one of my favorite Whitney Houston songs, I was a one-hit wonder. I kept getting requests from the audience. There was even a man in the audience who wanted to sing a duet, and we sang a horrible rendition of "Up Where We Belong." I finally exhausted most of the songs I knew and retired for the evening.

The next morning would demand my attention for the work I had set out on the trip to do. I had a good time the night before, but as usual, grief was waiting for me in my room. After praying, spending time reading my Bible, and getting dressed, I pulled back the curtain in my room and the work began. I cried, I read, I wrote in my journal. I sat in a chair, got back into bed, walked out on the balcony, talked to the mirror, and allowed my mind to go free. Not knowing what to expect, I was committed to doing whatever I needed to do. I thought a lot about Leander, our marriage, the funerals, the hospital scenes, and how my life looked at that point.

I wrote in my journal with as much truth as I could muster, writing things like *Leander is not coming back. He is not on an extended business trip. He is dead and buried in Baton Rouge. I am sad. I am hurting. I am lonely. This isn't fair. There is a hole in my soul. I want him back and I know he is not coming back. I am not ready for this. This is not the way my life is supposed to be right now. This was not the plan we had for our life. I want to grow old with Leander. We are supposed to hold hands and walk through life for 50 years. My dreams are shaken by my reality. I miss him so much. My feet are cold and he is not here to warm them. I want to feel his arms around me and his love connected to mine. What am I going to do now???*

I fell asleep, then tossed, turned, and woke up several times during the night. I was a mess. I walked the crowded square feet of my stateroom, bawled my eyes out, and tried to pull it back together to think complete thoughts. The next day, I stayed in the room and continued to work on myself. On the rare occasion of feeling a hunger pang, I ordered room service. But that was a wasted order because I had no desire to eat. I could feel that progress was being made. I was not in a sea of sadness, but in an arena of discovery. Finally, I could look in the mirror and tell myself I was going to be OK. My new normal was being developed. The reborn Gwendolyn was beginning to emerge on the other side of grief, an evolution that has continued since that cruise.

After staying in my stateroom for what seemed like an eternity, I finally emerged. I cleaned myself up, changed my hair, put on makeup and a cute outfit, and reentered the world of the cruise. Amazingly, I enjoyed the remainder of the cruise. I participated in some of the activities. I remember learning to make a gecko out of beads and safety pins. I even got off the ship at a couple of the ports. I cheated in one of the ports by going to the post office, buying a calling card, finding a phone, and calling home. *Don't judge me too harshly—Rome wasn't built in a day.* I know I still have a lot of work to do on myself.

The final night of the cruise, I participated in a talent show with a live band. My new friends were there videotaping and taking pictures like proud parents. They were exceptionally proud when I won the talent show. Now that's a new normal!

Who are the authorities that decide what normal is? We have all developed lifestyles and patterns of living that suit us just fine. What works for one person or one family might drive another person or family totally insane. Yet we often feel that we should copy someone else's idea of normal. We then enter into unnecessary compromise and if we are not careful will lose our sense of who we are. What is normal for you? What was your life like prior to the loss you have experienced? Has there been an interruption in your life? What responsibilities have you assumed that were previously the function of your dearly departed loved one? Life continues on in the absence of our loved ones, even though their earthly activities immediately cease. However, there is a reality not to be denied. If they were employed, their employer will soon refill the position. If they participated in the day-to-day activities in the home, someone will have to fulfill the roles that are now left vacated by their death.

In some instances, those of us who remain must readjust our lives to take care of ongoing or unfinished business. In other words, be prepared for normal to change when you lose a loved one. When Leander died, I suddenly had to respond by taking on many responsibilities that had previously been handled by him. We were fortunate in that while we had a joint bank account, I had an individual account as well. This would serve to be a plus in many ways. I have spoken with so many women who at the death of their husbands had never written a check, paid bills, or used a credit card. They did not know how to transact business. I thank God this was not the case for me, but I had my share of trials and inconveniences due to improper planning for this inevitable event.

While I'd been married before, I always had maintained a fair amount of financial independence. The day Leander died our family experienced not only physical loss but financial loss as well. Leander's affairs were not in order. I am sure he had no idea his death would occur December 6, 2001. I know he loved me and wanted to provide for our family. He just didn't have enough time to make sure this would occur.

I take partial responsibility for his business affairs not being in order. I did not want to have the discussion of preparing for death. I was a newlywed. We were fairly young. I thought we had more time. We had no warning. There were several times he would approach the subject of life insurance and his wishes for his last days, and I did not want to think about it let alone talk about it.

May I give you, the reader of this book, some strong advice? Get your business straight NOW! Make sure everything, all the paperwork regarding illness (whether prolonged or brief), is in order.

This includes power of attorney, living trust, will, and so forth. Get legal and financial advice regarding life insurance, retirement funds, social security, bank accounts, and joint or individual property. Life can end so suddenly and that is tragic enough without having to worry about mounting medical bills, funeral expenses, and living expenses. This advice is not just for survivors, it is for everyone. Take care of your own business. Be sure you have prepared for the ones you will leave behind. After Leander's death I immediately made certain that my family would be provided for in the event of my passing, and that my death will not be a burden on anyone.

After we muddled through final arrangements, three funerals, and finally made it back home, my house and my life seemed empty. Since our marriage, Leander and I had been almost inseparable. And now I had to learn to live without him. Having experienced the death of my husband, I have realized that life as I knew it would never be the same. My life as part of a happy couple is over. His input has ended. There were so many things that he enjoyed doing like grocery shopping, getting my car washed, filling my tank with gas, barbecuing, fixing special meals to surprise me, and the list goes on. What about all the things we enjoyed doing together: traveling, shopping, going for walks, driving to romantic getaways, going on lunch dates? I know I can do all these things without him, but it's not the same. How am I supposed to live without him? How will we make it through the holidays, birthdays, Phil's graduation from high school? What would I do on our anniversary? Would I ever be able to prepare his favorite meal again?

All of these questions didn't arrive in perfect succession as they are listed here. They arrived as life continued on. There was no way I could have thought of them immediately following his death. I could not have predicted my response to this turn of events. All I know is my life is forever changed. Suddenly and abruptly! Most times it's hard to remember the way it was. Grief is tricky. I still don't understand it. All I know is grief will deliver you into a state of being that is hard to explain or understand. Because of its elusive nature and individual response, not one of us knows how it will affect us and what our response will be until we are in the moment. I caution you not to be too literal about grief. Read, yes read what the researchers and prolific writers have documented on the subject. But know that grief has its way with us in an individual manner. I have spoken with several persons in different stages of grief and each one has expressed his or her dilemma associated with grief. None has been able to directly pinpoint an exact measurement or calculation of feelings and emotions through the experience of grief. While there are many similarities in varied individuals and their grieving processes, most agree that grief is individual.

For instance, my maternal grandfather died near Christmas one year. I never met him. He died before I was born. But as a child I came to know through my mother's actions that my grandfather loved Christmas music, particularly "Silent Night." This was evidenced by the fact that my mother would sing and play this song on the piano, crying all the while. This was not just in December, but also sometimes in April or July. As we got older, we realized Mom was remembering and grieving. There are countless untold stories of those who have experienced loss and their numerous ways of grieving and coping. These stories might seem strange and unconventional to others, but they are real for those of us who live these occurrences.

What I thought was normal is not normal anymore. The death of my husband has changed everything. I became a widow six weeks prior to my fiftieth birthday, and I was not prepared for this life change. It would be enough of a life change to turn fifty! The death of my husband, lover, friend, and partner in ministry abruptly altered my life, my love, and my happiness. What is normal for me? These days normal is just being able to get up in the morning and have rational thoughts. Normal is making it through a week without waking up at 4:28 AM feeling sad and lonely. Normal is booking a vacation and actually going—alone. Normal is choosing life and making every moment count. I have come to grips with the fact that life as I once knew it, is no more. I don't spend a lot of time focusing on what normal is and isn't. I just thank God every day when I wake up. I ask the Lord to guide me through the day as I live life *one day at a time*. I would like to think I am successfully moving beyond grief. I know I have joy because I have strength. The joy of the Lord is my strength.

Taking Self from the Shelf

This section is primarily for widows. Those who have lost a husband and need to get back in touch with who they are, might find this part very helpful. Perhaps prior to marriage there were dreams, goals, and ambitions that were delayed or denied for the sake of family. Perhaps as the marriage developed, the ambitions of the now deceased spouse were placed in the number one position. I know this is particularly true for some wives as they take a back seat position to allow their husbands to move forward. Well, now it's time to think about y-o-u. I don't suggest jumping into anything too quickly, but I suggest using this time as an opportunity to reflect on some of the things that may have been delayed or denied as you became a bride/groom, wife/husband, mother/father, and grandmother/grandfather. Many women have put their hopes, desires, and dreams on the shelf to become Mrs. _____. This is not the case for me. In doing several workshops for widows across the U.S. in the recent past, I have discovered that becoming a widow is for some a very tragic time in our lives, but becoming what we are destined to be is a blessing. God has a plan for our lives. The death of a spouse in not a joyous event, but the surviving spouse has not been given a death sentence. In fact, the message for the surviving spouse is LIVE. As the grieving subsides, pay close attention to the inner nudging of your heart. You may discover or rediscover interests that you now have time to explore.

The following five exercises are to encourage self-reflection and stimulate your thoughts for a new beginning. You must learn to think about and take care of you. I hope you are beyond the extreme sadness that may have been caused by loss. If you are, you will get the most out of this activity. If you are not, feel free to come back to this exercise at another time. Take a moment now—pause and reflect on your life. You are still alive. God has a purpose and plan for your life. If you have recently experienced the loss of a loved one, I am so sorry. The activity does not take the loss lightly. Take into consideration that as your life continues there is opportunity to expand your horizons and grow as a person. This is an extreme moment in your history; however, it is also a crossroad. If you have not experienced a loss, completing this exercise could add a new dimension to your life now.

Exercise #1
Can you think of anything that you have always wanted to do? For instance: start a business, go back to school, take an art class, write a book, travel, and so forth. Write your ideas in the space provided.

_____

_____

_____

_____

_____

_____

Exercise #2
Now, in the next few lines that are provided, write down what prevents you from doing those things now. For instance: fear, money, time, and so forth. Also write why these things should continue to be an obstacle for you.

Note: By doing the above exercise you may have found that your excuses are not valid, and there are some things you can begin doing.

Exercise #3

Make a few promises to yourself. Think about some things you can do for yourself. These things have no obstacles. Perhaps you need to exercise—then go for a walk. Perhaps you need to lose weight—eat less. Maybe you want to start the "new you" by getting a new look and a makeover—call Oprah or do it yourself. Look at exercise #1 and see if now would be a good time to plan something new. You must keep whatever promise/s you make to yourself. For some of us this is difficult. In my case, I have always been a caregiver and have taken good care of everyone but myself. So I have promised to take care of myself, lose weight, eat and live healthy, vacation in wonderful places, write several books, and go back to school.

What about you? Are you ready? Use the space below to write the promise/s you will make to you.

Action

Now, take one more step. Transfer the promises to a note card or piece of paper and put it where you will see it often. This will serve as your reminder. Title this card Promises to myself. Now you must immediately research the items, placing names, phones numbers, and an attainable time to complete on them.

Don't be too hard on yourself if you have to adjust the times to complete. If you have to adjust them more than twice you may need to give yourself more time to heal, then try them again.

You've heard the saying: "You can't take care of anyone else if you're not taking care of yourself." While traveling by plane you will hear the following instructions: *"In the case of an emergency an oxygen mask will come from over your seat. If you are traveling with small children or others that need assistance, place the mask over your mouth first then assist the others who cannot help themselves."* Take care of yourself.

CHAPTER 7

Promoting a Healthy You

AFTER LEANDER DIED, I made unhealthy, unwise decisions on how to use my time. I immediately shifted into a workload I knew he would have disapproved of. I have been a workaholic all my life. I thrive on having too many irons in the fire. When I met Leander, we had many discussions regarding this, and I promised him I would do better. He also convinced me that spending time with him was more fun and valuable. While in Omaha I had a home office. This room was across the hall from our bedroom. On too many occasions to count, Leander would knock on the door, turn off the lights or unplug equipment to get me to stop working after the hours had grown too long.

Shortly after Leander's death, I began working extremely long hours in the office and continued to work after arriving at home. I converted part of my bedroom into an office. I soon bought a laptop computer and this removed further barriers to my ability to work. I would work while waiting for Phil to get out of school, while I was getting my hair done, or on every trip whether business or pleasure. Work became my coping mechanism. Using the computer decreased my physical activity. This caused weight to increase in areas of my body that I did not even know existed. I also stopped paying attention to what I was eating. My way of ignoring feelings and my need to grieve was to keep busy. Activity will drown the pain for a moment, but as I've said earlier in this book, grief is always waiting for you when you stop.

Most of us can benefit from taking a good look at how we are living our lives, and then explore ways to gain a better quality of life. This could involve decisions to make some life changes. Our patterns of eating, thinking, working, and playing all come to mind when choosing to live a healthier lifestyle. Leander's death weight was three hundred and thirteen pounds. He suffered from diabetes, high blood pressure, heart disease, stress, and many other ailments unknown to me. I am sure that his numerous conditions attributed to his untimely demise. There are lifestyle choices we can make that increase our quality of life. Studies prove that people who select a plan for healthy eating, regularly exercise, consume low to moderate amounts of alcohol, abstain from substance abuse, and keep stress to a minimum live longer, healthier lives. My parents are a prime example. Mom is eighty-five and dad is eighty-six. They will soon celebrate fifty-seven years of marriage. They are in good health and still live a very active and independent lifestyle. *I'm sure glad I inherited those genes.* They are my living proof that healthy lifestyle, healthy relationship, and love of the Lord equal a long life.

Long life may not be everyone's ultimate goal, but how about enjoying the life you have while you have it?

Flying Solo

I am the only one left.
I Kings 19:10

I married for the first time five days after my seventeenth birthday. I thought I was mature enough to handle the most intimate relationship known to humankind. At the time of Leander's death I had been in married relationships off and on for thirty-two of my forty-nine years. I have experienced every kind of pain imaginable in marriage. Domestic violence, verbal and physical abuse, dishonesty, distrust, being cheated on, and financial ruin, to name a few. Finally, with Leander, I felt that God had placed the right man in my life but now he is gone. I am relational. I like being married. I like belonging. And now, I am flying solo. This would also be the first time in my life I had not initiated the end of a relationship. I didn't want him to leave. I wanted him to stay, but it was out of my hands. Out of my control. I buried the love of my life. What am I supposed to do now?

The answer to that question woke me up one morning a few months after Leander died. I looked at the clock and it was around three o'clock. This was my first clue to this not being a Leander moment, but a Gwendolyn moment. The words that came into my spirit and imagination were:

You are alive.

Live.

This message rang loud and true to my spirit before coming to grips with grief on the cruise. This message was the truth. I wasn't excited about the message when I first sensed it. My life had just been eternally altered. I would need to find a way to live without Leander. I would have to restructure my way of thinking, living, and being as a couple, to thinking as an individual. I no longer had someone with whom to share my deepest feelings and emotions. There was no one to bounce ideas off of. My partner, lover, and friend was gone and was not coming back. What was I supposed to do?

Live because I am alive!

Five months after Leander died, I was in Phoenix at an AME conference. In attendance were pastors, ministers, and lay people, most of whom I had not seen since Leander's funeral. I remember a minister predicting I would be married again within six months. I was appalled at the time. I know he was trying to be kind and in his own way say that I should not be so sad. That life goes on. However, this was an obvious misstatement.

Statistically, women tend not to marry again soon after their husbands die. However, research has shown that a large percentage of *men* marry rather quickly after the death of a wife. I have my opinion of why this is. When a man has been married to a woman who keeps a good house, cooks, cleans, sews, and keeps his sexual appetite satisfied, it isn't long before he needs to replace those attributes. I often say if I had died instead of Leander, I am sure at least ten women would have followed him home from the cemetery vying to be the next Mrs. Coates. He might have married again in six months to a year just to keep the parade of women off his trail.

Flying solo can be lonely, but I think it is good to regroup before reengaging in relationship. Thank God for those who have found love again after the death of a spouse. It hasn't happened to me yet, but if God sends love my way again, I hope I'll be able to receive it.

Until then, God has given me peace as I learn to fly solo. This brings to mind a true story that I will share with you. My first experience being a passenger in a single-engine plane was in 1982. I worked part-time as a back-up singer for Jessy Dixon, a well-known gospel artist with multiple albums. As the Jessy Dixon Singers, we had a performance in Nacadocious, Texas. Jessy lived (and still does) in Chicago, while the band and some of the background singers lived in other parts of the country. On this trip to Texas, we would all meet at the Dallas-Fort Worth airport and travel to Nacadocious on what I called a toy plane. We were all in first class. There were only twelve seats on the plane, and one of them belonged to the pilot. Because this was a small plane, there was a weight limit for passengers and luggage, and each person and piece of luggage had to be weighed. If the weight exceeded the limitations for safe travel, something or someone would have to take a later flight.

We would discover how valid this weight restriction was two weeks later, when another gospel singer traveling in Texas did not adhere to the weight restrictions. Keith Green was killed on July 28, 1982 when the small plane he was traveling in crashed. Green had been flying and visiting friends. Two of Green's children, three-year-old Josiah and two-year-old Bethany, were also on board the plane, as was pilot Don Burmeister, friends John and Dede Smalley, and all six of their children. All the passengers were killed in the crash. Crash investigators determined that the aircraft was nearly 500 pounds (230 kg) overweight with twelve passengers and only six seats.

I have deduced from the above story that if you're weighed down with too much baggage you can crash. I am recommitting to a self-made rule to regularly weigh the stuff I allow to enter my life, my mind, and my psyche. As I embark on this new life, new beginning, and new phase, it is necessary for me to unload many things, items, and even some people in order to have a balanced take-off and flight.

One Sunday afternoon about five months after Leander died, I unloaded some excess baggage. Without knowing the ramifications at the time, I emptied the closets of Leander's clothing, personal effects, and other reminders that would lead one to believe he was just on a business trip. I had just come home from church and had no idea this would be the day I'd move his things. It all started because I said to myself, "I need more closet space." The next thing I knew I was pulling Leander's clothes out of the closet, and filling boxes with clothing, shoes, books, and other items belonging to him that obviously he would no longer need.

I must have been making quite a bit of noise because Phil and LaNicia came running down the hall to see what was going on. They were traumatized to see Leander's things being moved with such intensity, yet they knew they'd better move quickly if they wanted to preserve anything. They rescued a few items they would like to keep and the rest was boxed and moved to the garage. I did not know this at the time, but this was a very therapeutic moment for me. I probably should have removed his things in a more civil manner, but just moving them at all was a good thing. I have since been informed that it is good to move the deceased clothing within three to six months—no longer than one year after the death. It would take another three months for me to move Leander's things out of the garage. I called Salvation Army and had a truck pick up his things when no one was home. On the day the truck was coming, I left home and left the boxes in front of the garage. It was easier for all of us that way.

The smell of his cologne was still in some of his clothes. I would occasionally walk in the closet just to remember his smell. There are some changes I am sorry I hastily made. His pillow also had the scent of his favorite fragrance on it and I soon replaced the pillow. While he was in the hospital, I recorded a new message using my voice on his voicemail. I later regretted erasing his voice so suddenly. This would be another source of sadness. I miss his warm, deep, melodious voice. No one can say, *Gwendolyn,* like Leander. I also got rid of his old Ford Taurus wagon that we affectionately referred to as *Betsy*. None of us could drive it without an avalanche of memories and tears.

In 2003 we moved from the house in Kent. The day we moved the wind was very high, and each time we opened the door to take more things out of the house, a strong wind would blow the door shut. We joked that Leander was in the wind, trying to prevent us from leaving the house he provided for us. Leaving was a good thing to do. We left behind several traces that would prevent new growth. We found the strength to enter a new season and a new phase in our lives.

I would like to share a final thought from the cruise to Alaska. One of the most incredible moments aboard the Norwegian Cruise Line, *Spirit,* was when we came into close proximity of the Sawyer Glacier. The magnificence of this natural splendor was breathtaking to say the least. Once it was announced on the public address system that we would be entering into the area of the glacier, everyone began finding the most appropriate places to behold this majestic brilliance. One of the phenomenons associated with this natural wonder is when the snow transforms into ice and the ice falls into the water creating an iceberg. These icebergs float in the water and because of oxidation cause the water to turn emerald green. I was blessed to have a front row seat for viewing by going to the balcony of my stateroom. While there I created lasting memories by taking several pictures of this evolving and ever-changing glacier. I was able to observe several splashes in the water created by the casting off of ice from the glacier.

It didn't take me long to turn these events into a life lesson. I garnered from the splashing of the ice that had been cast off from the glacier that in life we have many things growing in our minds. We become and stay healthy if we allow the natural casting off of the things that we no longer have use for. I would like to think that our discarded troubles oxidize and create something wonderful. I was able to observe several passengers aboard the ship who had the same view as I from their balconies. Interestingly, I noted that no one focused on the discarded icebergs for long because the brilliance of the glacier that was constantly reforming, reshaping, and recreating was the main event. This made me think about life and how our lives are constantly reforming, reshaping, and recreating. Each time I looked in the direction of the glacier, I was ever more grateful to see that no matter how much unusable ice was cast into the sea, the glacier remained intact and kept its form. In those moments I thanked God that as I cast off things in my life that are no longer usable, I will be intact and I will keep my form. I then began imagining that each iceberg that floated in the water represented my cast off fears, worries, problems, pain, and issues. What a good thought, because now I was able to see the crystal clear emerald water that now represented the beauty of my past.

I have said goodbye to a lot of memories. I have released a lot of anger and pain. I have signed up for my own forgiveness ceremony. I think I am ready to say hello to a new life . . . *flying solo.*

PART 3

Spiritual Strength for a Hurting Soul

CHAPTER 8

Help Me Make It Through the Night

> *"I am with you always, even to the end of the age." Amen.*
> MATTHEW 28:20

THE END OF THE DAY can be the most precarious time. The phones have stopped ringing, the television is turned off, visitors have gone home, family members are in their separate rooms, and the night has come. There is no one to talk to, no one to lean on, and no one to keep your feet warm. No one is there to gain strength from. Your pattern and routine have succumbed to the reality of being alone.

Everything is still and I am alone with my thoughts. My thoughts plague me. I am alone in the bed Leander and I once shared. The reality of his death continues to overshadow me. I am alone. I don't want to forget him, but now I remember his death and not his life. I am not going to feel sorry for myself. The pain of my reality becomes larger than life when nighttime comes.

At night I really feel alone.
At night I feel depressed.
At night I feel neglected.
At night I feel discouraged.

At night I sum up the day.
I am lonely.
I want companionship.
My body craves the love we once shared.
I miss Leander.
I no longer hear his voice. His laughter has been silenced.
Leander's bigger-than-life personality is gone.
When I close my eyes I see the hospital scene.
When I am in my bedroom, I try to reenact his last moments in the house.
Though the bloodstain has been removed from the carpeted floor in our bedroom, the floor speaks to me. This is the spot where he suffered alone.
I wake up because I need him.
I need to feel his presence.
I know I cannot go to him and he cannot come to me.
I want to scream.
I want to cry.
I cry.
I don't feel any better.

This is how I have felt, night after night. I have not always been able to spiritualize my grief. All of us, no matter how strong we are, need strength for the journey.

God can you hear me?
Speak to me Lord.
Minister to my wounded spirit.
I cry out to You because I love You and trust You.
Lord, please be my shoulder.
No one understands my pain but You.
Take control of my mind and my thoughts.
I need sleep.
Are my children all right?
We need courage, Lord.
Lord, please be my strength.

From the moment I realized Leander would not be keeping our lunch date, until even now, I am so glad I have strong faith and a relationship with my Lord and Savior, Jesus Christ. Without a close personal relationship with the Lord, the pain of Leander's death would have been unbearable. I am grateful for the immediate peace God gifted me with in the midst of a traumatic situation. I know it was God who gave me courage and strength to keep a level head during a chaotic season. In my despair, I called on the Lord and He heard me.

> *I called on the Lord in distress; The Lord answered me*
> *and set me in a broad place. The Lord is on my side;*
> *I will not fear. What can man do to me?*
> Psalm 118: 5-6

I gave my heart to the Lord when I was seven years old. When I asked to be baptized, I was told I was too young. In the Missionary Baptist Church I was raised in, the pastor believed a child should be twelve years old before he or she was baptized. However, our church bent the rules for me. I loved the Lord and everyone knew it. I was baptized. I had an encounter with the Holy Spirit when I was thirteen years old. It was then that I sensed a ministry calling on my life. I had sensed it for around five years by that time, but didn't know how to express my feelings. This would present a problematic situation for my family. I was a girl who felt called by God to teach, preach, and sing God's Word. To some degree I was discouraged, although at the same time, I was cultivated as a youth speaker, Sunday School teacher, and vocalist. Some might say I didn't have a childhood. But I say I had the best childhood. As I look back now, I am so grateful the Lord chose me at an early age.

I know the Lord loves me and has a wonderful plan for my life. If you are reading this right now, the same is true for you.

> *For I know the plans I have for you, says the Lord, plans for welfare and not for evil, to give you a future and a hope.*
> Jeremiah 29:11(RSV)

In our most critical points in life, it is so important that we know we are not alone.

I will never leave you nor forsake you.
Hebrews 13:5b

What comforting words in the lonely hours of nighttime. Having a relationship with the Lord and having the Word of God in your heart become extremely important in times like these. There were days upon end when I found it difficult to pick up the Bible and read it. I have read the Bible many times before and have memorized many Scriptures. The Lord ministered to me from what was already in my heart.

Your Word I have hidden in my heart that
I might not sin against You.
Psalm 119:11

If you sense the need to accept Jesus as your Savior and Lord, now is the time to settle the matter. Ask God to speak to you as you read the following scriptures:

All have sinned and come short of the glory of God.
Romans 3:23

For the wages of sin is death, but the gift of God is
eternal life in Christ Jesus our Lord.
Romans 6:23

But God demonstrates His own love toward us,
in that while we were still sinners, Christ died for us.
Romans 5:8

God demonstrates His love for us through Jesus' death, which paid the penalty for our sins.

For "whoever calls on the name of the Lord shall be saved."
ROMANS 10:13

Just by asking God to save you, GOD WILL!

If you confess with your mouth the Lord Jesus and believe in your heart that God has raised Him from the dead, you will be saved. For with the heart one believes unto righteousness, and with the mouth confession is made unto salvation.
ROMANS 10: 9-10

The Scriptures are very plain. If you recognize that you are a sinner and need a saving relationship with Jesus Christ, confess and agree with God about your sins.

Make a promise to turn from your sins and turn to God. This is called repentance. Then ask Jesus to save you by His grace. Now you are ready to turn over the control of your life to Jesus. Let Jesus love you as no one else can. Let Him be your Lord and Savior.

You're ready. Pray this prayer and let the Lord lead and guide you into eternal life.

Lord, I am a sinner. I have done some things that I am not proud of. Please forgive me. Accept me as your child and I accept you as my Savior. I believe Romans 10: 9-10. Thank you for saving me. Amen.

If you prayed this prayer and really meant it, you are now saved. E-mail me at GAPPRAY@MSN.COM and let me know you just prayed this prayer. I will add you to our prayer list. Now you have something to do. Get excited and tell at least three people about this wonderful decision you have made today. Write the date down here _____ _____. This day is now as important as your birthday. Celebrate!

I pray you can find a place to worship that will encourage you as you grow on this new path. In the meantime, I encourage you to read the Book of John. Find and purchase a version of the Bible that you can easily understand. I personally recommend the Today's New International Version or New International Version Study Bible for easy understanding and clarity. I also highly recommend you get into a Bible study group. Not only will this provide companionship, you will be able to learn as you hear the thoughts and ideas of others as you grow in the Lord. If you really get excited and want to start your own Bible study group, I recommend *Experiencing God: Knowing and Doing His Will—Workbook* by Henry Blackaby, an interactive discipleship Bible study. Your local bookstore should have it or try Lifeway.com, Christianbook.com or Amazon.com.

Welcome to the family of faith.

God bless you as you grow in him.

I have had many lonely days and nights but I know God is with me. I have the assurance that I am never alone. Now you can make it through the night.

Remember:

- The Lord calms the storms in our lives.

> *Peace. Be still.*
> MATTHEW 4:39

- Trouble doesn't last always.

> *He restores my soul.*
> PSALM 23:3

- Trials make us strong.

> *Count it all joy when you fall into various trials.*
> JAMES 1:2

- Thank God, you are loved.

> *I love you with an everlasting love.*
> JEREMIAH 31:3

CHAPTER 9

Mourning to Dancing

GRIEF IS AN OVERWHELMING COMPANION. But the pain of grief does subside and eventually becomes a memory. I cannot pinpoint the day that it happened. I just know that one day I woke up with pep in my step. I felt like I had been on an extended vacation from reality and now I was coming back. The best analogy I can give is going to have dental treatment. When the doctor numbs the area of your mouth and gums that will be treated, the initial pain is from the needle issuing a numbing solution. Soon the pain of the needle subsides and numbness takes the place of the pain. During the dental procedure and for some time afterwards you will experience numbness in that area of your mouth. After leaving the dental office you are able to participate in normal activities. As you do, you notice slight limitations in talking, eating, and putting on lipstick because of the effects of the numbing. You are able to function but with slight limitations. These limitations can go unnoticed. Sometime later, you will experience a tingling sensation because the feeling is coming back into the formerly numbed area. As the numbness subsides you might experience slight pain in the area that was treated. The dentist may have even given you a prescription to ease your pain. In a few days, without warning, the pain will go away.

You will never forget the pain you have experienced due to the death of a loved one. The pain is real, not a figment of your imagination. But thank God the day will come when the pain is just a memory. The numbing effect of grief manifests itself in so many different ways. There were times when I began to believe that my attitude and psyche had permanently changed. And this is true, in some ways the effects of grief have changed me permanently. The positives changes have been that I am intentionally showing love and appreciation. I tell my family I love them more often, I value *real* friendships and I have a closer walk with the Lord. Because I have had a personal forgiveness ceremony, I have destroyed roots of bitterness that I harbored in my heart.

I don't know what is in my future. I just know that my future is in God's unchanging hands. The following is a scripture for meditations and reflection.

Psalm 30

I will extol You, O Lord, for You have lifted me up, and have not let my foes rejoice over me. O Lord my God, I cried out to You, and You healed me. O Lord, You brought my soul up from the grave; You have kept me alive, that I should not go down to the pit. Sing praise to the Lord, you saints of His, and give thanks at the remembrance of His holy name. For His anger is but for a moment, His favor is for life; weeping may endure for a night, but joy comes in the morning.

Now in my prosperity I said, "I shall never be moved." Lord, by Your favor You have made my mountain stand strong; You hid Your face, and I was troubled. I cried out to You, O Lord; and to the Lord I made supplication: "What profit is there in my blood, when I go down to the pit? Will the dust praise You? Will it declare Your truth? Hear, O Lord, and have mercy on me; Lord, be my helper!" You have turned for me my mourning into dancing; You have put off my sackcloth and clothed me with gladness, to the end that my glory may sing praise to You and not be silent. O Lord my God, I will give thanks to You forever.

CHAPTER 10

A New Beginning

I AM BLESSED TO HAVE LOVED and lived with Leander in my life. He and I experienced a great love relationship. Because of him, I know that I am capable of unconditional love. I miss him and he can never be replaced. I am on a new journey now. My life is beginning again. I have made great strides with the help of the Lord. I have come a long way and I know I have a long way to go. It is hard to think about moving on when the life you had was wonderful. It is also impossible to move forward while looking back. There is a new road ahead for each of us who has been on the journey through grief. I pray that everyone reading this book will trust God for every move.

For those who have lost a spouse through death, let God love you. By the grace of God, you are still alive. God has more for you to accomplish. There is healing available to you. You are not alone. When you are strong enough, reach out to others who experience loss. Your loss is not the last loss to be experienced. Death is occurring all around us everyday. As you recover, let your life exhibit the love of the Lord. You are now embarking on a new journey. Life is different, but life can be sweet. You can make it. This is a new beginning. Go ahead. Start the journey.

Want to know how to begin this journey?
One step at a time . . . . . .
God bless you. I wish for you peace, hope, joy, and love.

WHEN MORNING COMES

Darkness fills the empty space
Tears streaming down my face
The night engulfs me and surrounds me
How can I escape and be free?

Am I awake, is this a dream
It seems so real, reigns supreme
This is my life without the light
Every day is filled with night.

When morning comes, your path will be brighter
When morning comes your load will be lighter
Lift up your eyes to the breaking of dawn.
Peace, hope, joy, and love
When morning comes.

Discouraged by life's crushing blows
Unable to move, paralyzed by woes
Filled with doubt, gripped with grief
Disillusioned, broken, have no relief.

There is an answer, wait till the morning
Lift up your eyes to the breaking of dawn
The light of day heaven is sending
You will know when morning comes.

When morning comes your path will be brighter
When morning comes your load will be lighter
Lift up your eyes to the breaking of dawn.
Peace, hope, joy and love
When morning comes.

It starts with a whisper of light
Then grows to become so beautiful, bright
Darkness released, no more night

Morning is cheerful, prudent and wise
Morning is freedom, let it be your guide
Morning is light rescued from the night.

When morning comes your path will be brighter
When morning comes your load will be lighter
Lift up your eyes to the breaking of dawn
Peace, hope, joy, and love
When morning comes.

No more night—peace, hope, joy, and love.
Joy comes in the morning—peace, hope, joy, and love.
Peace, hope, joy, and love
When morning comes.

Written by Gwendolyn Phillips Coates
for Grateful,
1995 God Answers Prayer Records.

ORDER FORM

God Answers Prayer Ministries, Inc.
God Answers Prayer Records/Philabob Publishing

NAME:_____ PHONE _____

ADDRESS_____CITY_____STATE_____ZIP_____

	QUANTITY	TAPE	CD	TOTAL
Waiting on My Lunch Date $15.99/ea				
Wisdom and Grace Devotional Bible $25/ea				
It's Christmas Rejoice! Tape $8 CD $12				
Grateful tape $10 CD $15				
The Responsibility of Sharpskills CD $15				
			SUB TOTAL	
			GRAND TOTAL	

Make checks/money orders/cashiers checks payable to:

GAP Ministries, Post Office Box 1982, Renton, WA 98057-1682

☐ Visa ☐ MC ☐ Discover Acct #_____ EXP _____

Signature _____

www.gap-ministries.com